W9-CON-442

DATE DUE

WASN'T THE GRASS GREENER?

ALSO AVAILABLE IN BEELER LARGE PRINT BY
BARBARA HOLLAND

BINGO NIGHT AT THE FIRE HALL

WASN'T THE GRASS GREENER?

A Curmudgeon's Fond Memories

Barbara Holland

BEELER LARGE PRINT
Hampton Falls New Hampshire, 2000

Library of Congress Cataloging-in-Publication Data

Holland, Barbara.
    Wasn't the grass greener? : a curmudgeon's fond memories /
Barbara Holland.
    p.   cm.
    ISBN 1-57490-281-4 (alk. paper)
    1. United States—Social life and customs—1971- 2. United
States—Social life and customs—20th century. 3.
Nostalgia—United States. I. Title. II. Large type books.

E169.04. H644 2000
973.92—dc21   00-033732

Published in Large Print by arrangement with
Harcourt, Inc.

BEELER LARGE PRINT
is published by
Thomas T. Beeler, *Publisher*
Post Office Box 659
Hampton Falls, New Hampshire 03844

Typeset in 16 point Times New Roman.
Printed on acid-free paper and bound by
Sheridan Books in Chelsea, Michigan

For my grandmother,
with respect long overdue

Then every cross-bow had a string,
And every heart a fetter;
And making love was quite the thing,
And making verses better;
And maiden aunts were never seen,
And gallant beaux were plenty;
And lasses married at sixteen
And died at one-and-twenty.
Ay, those were golden days! The moon
Had then her true adorers;
And there were lyres and lutes in tune,
And no such thing as snorers.

-Edward Fitzgerald

Contents

INTRODUCTION

HERE WE ARE, ANOTHER THOUSAND YEARS OLDER, wiser, and happier.

Things have never been better. The American twentieth century has been one long revolution in the field of private happiness. Its early years brought us the radio, to drown out the voices in our heads, and revived the ancient Roman custom of bathing, with indoor plumbing and heated water, so that now the personal bathroom has replaced the crowded kitchen as the heart of domestic life. As the decades passed, triumph followed triumph. Pharmaceutical breakthroughs erased our existential despairs as well as our distracting euphorias. The painful path of true love was smoothed away, first by consensual and then by virtual sex. The Internet will educate our children to a brilliance never before imagined, and science has enriched our lives with power steering, cruise control, and the self-cleaning cat-litter pan.

Life is good.

Our discords have died away. The political left and right have mislaid their differences. World capitalism reigns unthreatened. The passionate marchers of labor unions, desegregation, segregation, women's rights, gay rights, Vietnam, love, disarmament, and nuclear power plants have laid aside their banners and settled down, all passion spent, to make a lot of money. Peace is with us.

Life is easy. We can simply drive up to a window, and either somebody will hand us a cooked hamburger or money will pour out of a slot in the wall. We no longer need to play games, dance, sing, or even talk, now that skilled professionals are paid to do it all for us on television.

We have more fun than any generation of mankind before us. Hundreds of cable channels and millions of videotapes, audiotapes, compact discs, and computer programs entertain us around the clock; joy, no longer dependent on other people or our unreliable selves, springs up at the touch of a button.

At millennium's end, we have achieved a kind of personal Nirvana here in America. Oddly, the favorite words of travel agents are "escape" and "getaway," but from what should we escape? Life is happiness indeed.

Only occasionally, here and there, the voice of the curmudgeon is heard in the land, peeping crossly for that which has been left back there by the roadside.

Never mind. There's always been someone like that. Always someone crying, "Wait! Turn around! Go back and see what it is. Maybe it's only a mitten some child has dropped, or a paper cup, but maybe its something we needed. Go back and look."

DOCTORS

WHEN I WAS A CHILD THE DOCTOR WAS GOD. LIKE God, in exchange for respect and obedience—"doctor's orders"—he guided us through the valley of the shadow, held out the hope of life eternal, and came when we summoned him, yea, even through snowstorms, to sit on the edge of our bed and lay his hand on our fevered brow.

Our parents were wise by definition but he was infallible by definition; "The doctor knows best" was an incantation you could lean on. We trusted him utterly. Like God, he was the safety net forever spread under our precarious lives. Like God, he was the powerful superparent standing backup behind our mortal parents, appearing as if by magic when our mother's remedies failed, black bag in hand: "Well, well, what seems to be the trouble? Let's have a look."

In the days before the all-purpose antibiotic, it was important for the doctor to figure out what ailed you, and this he did, not in the lab, but sitting on your bed. It was an art form as much as a science and a clever diagnostician was much admired. He touched your skin and lifted your eyelids and peered down your throat; he flexed your knees and elbows and thumped your back. He unbuttoned your pajamas and listened to your heart and lungs. His interest was inexpressibly comforting and most people felt better almost at once. Even if his bedside manner was brusque and his voice tired and impatient, that couldn't disguise the love he bore us. The love was implicit in his coming; why else would he be at our side? I'm sure I wasn't the only child who

1

wept upon learning that he charged money for his services, but even that didn't shake my faith in his love.

In nineteenth-century novels the heroine's grave condition was underlined by the number of doctor's visits per day. It's never clear exactly what he was *doing* on these visits, but visit he did, and often the languishing lady cheered up, sipped a little beef tea, and recovered. Back then, illness was a more personal matter. It was said that those with a "strong constitution" would pull through, while the naturally sickly and patients whose constitutions had been previously undermined would turn up their toes and die of a fever like Sweet Molly Malone. Even those who believed in germs didn't give germs much credit; violent emotional scenes or fits of passion might throw a person into a fatal fever, at least in novels. The doctor stood by, lending the constitution moral support, shoring it up with a change of air, a change of scene, an ocean voyage.

Temperament was a factor. Some patients, often young ladies disappointed in love, simply wasted away, while others went into a decline. Older men were more likely to be carried off by apoplexy, or sheer bad temper, and young men who read and studied too much were subject to death from brain fever. Many patients were described as having "taken to their beds," thus becoming bedridden; being bedridden was apparently a recognized disease in itself.

For the first half of the twentieth century, the doctor cured us with aspirin, orange juice, bed rest, and the laying-on of hands. If we worsened, he put us in a hospital where we stayed, complaining about the food, until he was quite satisfied with our condition. (Then he sent us bills, or sent them to our family if we'd perished, and the phrase "doctor's bills" rang ominously, and the impecunious often took years to pay them off.)

Medicine has made tremendous strides since then, and by rights we should worship our doctor more fervently than ever, but somehow we don't. He never comes to see us anymore. Sometimes he doesn't bother to discover personally exactly what's the matter by inspecting our ailing bodies; if for some reason he needs to touch us, he first puts on latex gloves and a mask. Then he writes a prescription that should cure whatever it is, and if that fails, he orders lab tests. He maketh us to fill out daunting piles of paper that look like tax forms. Rumors circulate about his income, comparable to sports stars'; sometimes we think he might be healing us as much for money as for love. He's a quitter, too, and when we seem really sick he thrusts us away from him, sends us off to a specialist we've never seen before. Indeed, we may never have seen our doctor himself—now called a health-care provider—before.

Back in 1990, a few people were suggesting that we take up some kind of national health insurance, like that provided by all other civilized countries, but the resulting outcry approached mass hysteria. It would mean the end of that warm, close, caring relationship between doctor and patient, so essential to therapy; it would mean we might see a doctor who didn't remember when we had chicken pox. The national-health movement slunk away with its tail between its legs, and the very next day was replaced by something called health maintenance organizations. Under these, assorted providers are assigned to groups of patients, and the less the providers do for the patients, the richer they get. Accountants decide what absolutely must be done and what can be skipped. Nobody complains about hospital food anymore; perhaps hospitals no longer need to serve food, since all the patients are sent home before dinnertime. Consumer advocates urge us to get tough with our provider organizations, demand our rights, and stomp out in a snit to try elsewhere, but this is a lot to ask when we're wobbly and feverish, or perhaps unconscious.

Since doctors no longer talk to us by phone, offering advice and consolation and prescriptions free of charge, some conscientious providers have now gone on-line, so we can share our ailment with our computer. ("If temperature is elevated, click here.")

It's lonelier to be sick now, and scarier than it used to be, and millions of us have turned our backs on the new doctors and searched out Chinese women with needles, massage therapists, manipulators of joints, chanters of mantras, and purveyors of roots and barks and herbs and essential unguents. They seem friendlier. The shamans and wiccans with cures from the woods and ditches are more reassuring than the doctor himself, who has turned so cold and uncaring and who may not be God after all.

In the great yellow fever epidemic in Philadelphia, in 1793, the famous Dr. Benjamin Rush saw well over a thousand patients, bearing the cure he'd invented and believed in passionately. His treatment consisted of ripping their guts out with mercury purges and draining off most of their blood. This savage remedy should have killed them all, even if they hadn't been already sick, but an astonishing number survived and flourished.

He had tremendous confidence and courage. He strode into their evil-smelling chambers and sat on their vomit-soaked beds and smiled and said, "You have nothing but a yellow fever."

Probably they trusted him. Probably they thought he

was God, and loved them, and it would be ungrateful and impious of them to die.

More of us stay alive today under the tender care of the antibiotics that replaced the doctor. We must learn to feel the same respect and trust for our bottle of pills, and smile weakly but gratefully at it when it comes to our bedside. Press it to our fevered brow, this pharmaceutical father figure squeezed into a plastic tube, with two refills and possible side effects but comforting, powerful, and wise. And probably very soon now medical science will have the bottle programmed to murmur, when we pry off the lid, "Well, well, what seems to be the trouble? Let's have a look."

WAR

DURING THE WAR IN THE PERSIAN GULF, BRIEF AS IT was, we heard a lot about psychological counseling for America's children, to help them cope with their anxieties. These weren't necessarily children with relatives in the line of fire, just plain children. Either we're raising a generation of crybabies or war just isn't much fun anymore.

If a quick glance back over world history shows us anything, it shows us that war was one of our most universal joys from our earliest beginnings, savored at every possible opportunity and even some quite incomprehensible ones, like the assassination of the Archduke Ferdinand, whomever he may have been. War buffs—and they are still legion—even relish the War of Jenkin's Ear. (The organ in question was lopped off by a Spanish coastguardsman in 1731, inspiring a war between England and Spain that segued into the War of the Austrian Succession. Surely you remember *that* one?)

The Old Testament consists almost entirely of the smiting of enemies. The 18th psalm exults:

> I have pursued mine enemies, and overtaken them: neither did I turn again till they were consumed. I have wounded them that they were not able to rise: they are fallen under my feet. For thou hast guided me with strength unto the battle: thou hast subdued under me those that rose up against me. Thou hast also given me the necks of mine enemies, that I might destroy them that hate me. They cried, but there was none to save them: even unto the Lord, but he answered them not. Then did I beat them small as dust before the wind: I did cast them out as dirt in the streets.

There speaks a happy psalmist.

The miraculous conversion of the emperor Constantine, which brought the eastern Roman Empire and a lot of the rest of the world under Christianity's wing, was brought on by a blazing cross in the sky over the message, "In this sign, conquer." This didn't mean he was going to conquer sin or personal frailty or anything wimpy like that. It meant he would mash his enemies into applesauce under his boots, and he did.

In many times and places, war was considered the only proper, dignified occupation for a young man and avoiding it such a character flaw that his own mother stopped speaking to him. War was a major part of male identity and a basic distinction between men and women, men and boys. The word *glory* was bandied about, a word rarely applied to, say, stock-trading, and it was heady stuff. "War," wrote the philosopher William James ruefully, "is the romance of history, and the possibility of violent death the soul of all romance."

Success in war was the only success that counted; failure was a disgrace to be wiped out only by starting another war and winning it. Courage on the field of battle was the true measure of a man. "Come home with your shield or upon it," said the mothers of Sparta. Cowardice could be expunged only by immediate suicide; ancient Romans and modern Japanese disemboweled themselves, and up until yesterday British officers who'd dishonored the regiment were handed a pistol and left alone to "do the right thing."

Smiting enemies has always been so admired that, unlike medicine or archaeology, it entitled its successful practitioners to become kings, emperors, and presidents of the United States like Washington, Jackson, William Henry Harrison, Taylor, Grant, and Eisenhower. The election of President Clinton in spite of his distaste for the Vietnam War speaks of war's sad decline in prestige.

Warfare was fun for those who took active part in it, combining the icy thrills of danger with the warming glow of comradeship and the possibility of medals or plunder or a prisoner whose family would ransom him. It was fun for those who stayed home, inflating the civilians to three times their normal size with pride in the reflection of national valor. It stimulated the ladies. "She loved me for the dangers I had pass'd," said Othello. In all times and places, the war hero drew feminine admirers like ants to a picnic. (The females of most lesser species seem to feel the same way.) Even the sight of the uniform, symbolic of possible future heroship, was exciting, and young ladies in Jane Austen would look at no man not an officer.

March tempo, the dance music and threat display of the male, raised everyone's pulse rate. It stiffened the sinews, summoned up the blood. War was pure adrenaline—Once more unto the breach, dear friends! Cry God for Harry, England, and St. George! It was the chief or maybe the only source of patriotism, and many a politician, from prehistory up to this morning, unified a discontented citizenry by pointing out a national danger and declaring war on it. The malcontents promptly stopped complaining about taxes, closed ranks, and took up arms, shoulder to shoulder, to save the homeland.

In former days much depended on the individual's strength and skill with battle-ax or longbow or whatever the local culture wielded, and this was a cherished source of individual pride. Then these personal talents were replaced by sophisticated weaponry, but at least in the beginning that was fun too. A fighter pilot could identify with the speed and power of his plane; a bombardier could feel personally responsible for that bone-shaking boom and all that broken glass and flying masonry.

World War II was fun. From a kid's-eye view, my view, a kid in Washington, D.C., where air-raid drills were serious stuff and our schools were full of exiled princesses, World War II was the greatest game of all, the best of all possible toys. Anxiety? What anxiety? Back then, children read and were read to, and the first great lesson of kids' books was that the dragon never eats the prince. We were good, Nazis were bad. Hitler was crazy. We would win. In the meantime, all over the neighborhood the six-to twelve-year-old world pitched in to help with what was called the war effort.

The grown-ups' agenda for us was slightly different from our own. Grown-ups wanted us to go from door to door soliciting War Bond pledges. They wanted us to drag our express wagons through the streets collecting old newspapers and twisted eggbeaters and rusty potato peelers, weapons guaranteed to drive the Axis powers whimpering back to their lairs. Mothers wanted us to eat the things they grew in the backyards—kale and Swiss chard and other insults—because kale consumption would bring the *Luftwaffe* down in flames.

This was nonsense, and we knew it. We had other plans. We knew what victory required of us, and it had nothing to do with vegetables.

Victory required us to lie on our backs in the grass all afternoon watching for German bombers cruising over Connecticut Avenue toward the White House and alert the authorities (I think we had a number to call) in the nick of time. We had charts of silhouettes, our planes and theirs, and kept them propped on our chests. The sky was thick with planes, the grass was thick with kids, but I, always terminally nearsighted, was the only one who ever actually spotted any German bombers.

Victory required us to dig trenches across people's lawns to impede the movements of enemy infantry through northwest Washington. It required us to catch spies. The Rogerses were spies. They never had candy at Halloween, always a dead giveaway, and the bushes around their downstairs windows were overgrown to hide their evil activities. As evening fell, we wriggled through the forsythia tangle and peered into their lighted living room, waiting for them to show their true colors by speaking German into a shortwave radio.

Mr. and Mrs. Rogers sat and read throughout their

tranquil evenings, and their dog snoozed on the rug, and outside we got pins and needles in our feet and spiders down our necks, but war, as Sherman said, is hell, and we endured until long past bedtime, night after night.

Aside from waves of school-borne propaganda, nobody told us much, leaving us free to invent our own war. We hadn't the foggiest notion where Germany was, for instance; it could have been in Delaware —wherever *that* was. At school, half the regular teachers had vanished into the services or lucrative war work, and the bewildered crew that replaced them may not have known much more than we did. Music class, always our main resource for history, geography, poetry, and religion, was our strongest information link. In a glorious jumble that included martial airs from all previous wars—"Marching to Pretoria," "Marching through Georgia," "When Johnny Comes Marching Home," etc.—we sang "The Marine's Hymn" and "Praise the Lord and Pass the Ammunition," and we really put our backs into them. We also sang a hideous government-issue ditty that began

You can defend America!
Nobody will if you don't!
Clean up the nation from bottom to top
Start with yourself in the home and the shop.

We sneered at the notion of Hitler shrinking terrified from our spotless floors and checkout counters. We knew him better than that—he was made of sterner stuff. But so were we.

We prepared for invasion. The boys practiced hand-to-hand combat; the girls constructed elaborate booby traps from clothesline and coat hangers, which occasionally netted the mailman. We stashed crackers and raisins in the vacant lot, prepared to hide out there and commit sabotage when our houses were occupied by enemy troops. There we dug holes in which we planned to crouch until time to creep out and poison the Nazi general's orange juice; we brewed the poison from cigarette butts and laundry soap. We wrote out secret codes, memorized them, and ate the paper. We communicated in invisible ink which, alas, remained permanently invisible. The better to penetrate enemy lines unrecognized, we practiced a kind of imitation German, full of *achtungs* and spit. Those of us old enough to own jackknives whittled scrap lumber into guns that would surely, at least from a distance, fool entire enemy regiments into surrender. The rest of us made bows for shooting arrows tipped with purloined lethal substances—rubbing alcohol, ammonia, melted aspirin.

From morn till night we were busy and happy and out from underfoot. It was a wonderful toy and a glorious war, and while we rejoiced in victory when it came, life seemed savorless for a long time afterward.

They don't make 'em like they used to. Wars have gone sadly downhill.

Many aficionados managed to enjoy the Cold War, even lacking as it was in stirring songs. It kept their minds off their own lives and gave them something to blame for whatever went wrong. They thought about the Communist threat morning, noon, and night, and its collapse has left a painful vacuum in their days. The possibility of nuclear annihilation and the end of all life on earth wasn't a pleasure, exactly, but it was definitely a thrilling thought; high stakes indeed; an ultimate frisson; and certainly it beat staying alive under a different economic system.

Suburban folk spent happy hours digging holes in their backyards, just as we dug them in vacant lots in my childhood, and stocking them with canned goods and rifles with which to defend their canned goods from the neighbors. A river of hardware-heavy movies and spy novels kept our martial spirits up, but somehow Korea and Vietnam, the hot wars imbedded in the Cold War, were a disappointment. When Johnny came marching home from Vietnam, instead of showering him with roses we suspected him of festering neuroses. Sometimes the whole war seemed like a neurosis.

Glory was leaking out of our ancient sport.

Part of the problem was our arsenal. It seemed to be getting bigger than we were, possibly with an independent agenda of its own. It wasn't lovable any more. Maybe a B-52 was never as intimate as a broadsword, but a person could figure out how it worked and relate to it; it's hard to relate to a nuclear warhead. Besides, our new stuff wasn't as useful as we'd hoped. Most men were, and still are, proud of the sheer size of the Pentagon budget and the sheer scope of what we could do, but we never seem to have room to do it without blowing up the neighboring countries and possibly ourselves to boot, and what fun is a toy too big to play with? Indeed, some of the toy's are almost no fun at all, and the thought of meadows seeded with invisible, permanent land mines waiting to blow the legs off children yet unborn is hard to enjoy, even if you put them there yourself.

We began to notice that a change had come over the smiting business. In its older, purer form it was fought at ground level, by opposing armies on battlefields. Where they passed by on their way to or from the battle, they might raid the barn and henhouse and ride off with the horses, but civilians beyond the line of march could go about their business, scolding their children and working to get the harvest in. When the war was over, the houses and gardens were still around, and the cathedral and the roads and the marketplace, and life went on. Now war turns ugly on the bystanders and blows holes in the infrastructure.

The Persian Gulf War raised a few diehard fans to a fever pitch of patriotism and provided some of the most exciting television footage since the *Challenger* blew up, but it worried the children and even some of the grownups weren't impressed. They were heard muttering unpatriotically that the Kuwaitis were scum-buckets and who cared if whatsisname ate them for lunch. Some found our oil interests a less heart-lifting, song-inspiring cause than, say, stopping Hitler, or even adding all Gaul to the Roman Empire. (President Bush said it wasn't really about oil at all, but to cheer us up: ". . . and by God, we're over the Vietnam syndrome at last!")

Since then, miniwars have been popping up every-where like a hatch of fleas and the decline accelerates. If the weapons have grown too impersonal to love, the causes have grown indecently personal. All pretense of ideological or patriotic content has been thrown to the winds. Turf wars involving whole countries are fought between rival honchos and their extended families, like the street wars of rival drug dealers. Whoever's temporarily on top gets to steal anything that's left to steal. Other wars are fought because people suddenly realize that, for obscure historical or ethnic reasons, they really, *really* hate the neighbors and want to inflict hideous, prolonged pain upon them and their children, by hand. This must be great fun for the people doing the inflicting or they wouldn't go on doing it, but to the onlookers it just isn't the same as the gallant and glorious warfare of old. Still other wars seem to consist entirely of roving teenagers with fancy weaponry they picked up from the ditches where the grown-ups left it; their goal is to wipe out the population and steal everything and then knock down the buildings they used to call home.

Most of these new wars involve people who don't even wear *uniforms*. They don't have parades with fifes and drums, or get medals, or puddle up at the mention of cause and country. Probably tender maidens don't shower them with flowers when they march home victorious; probably they don't even *march*. What fun can they possibly be having?

It's sad. War was a central pleasure and pastime through all human history, and we've spoiled it for ourselves. If we're going to make it through the next thousand years, we'll need to think of something equally riveting to take its place. Soccer matches and computer games try hard, but something deep in the manly soul misses the dizzying pungent smell of risk and the roll of drums.

SUNTANS

THE IDEAL COLOR OF HUMAN SKIN HAS LONG BEEN A subject of debate. In any given generation a dozen or so young English girls have the skin usually described as "porcelain," of a pearly transparency with undertones of pink, and this is much praised but highly perishable and requires constant tending. At the other end of the color spectrum, some Africans are actually black, a flat, uniform, matte black, impervious to late nights and acne, which they dramatize by being tall and narrow and wearing bright red and yellow sarongs. You can admire them in *National Geographic,* but you don't see them much around here, since they'd rather jump down a volcano than pack up their cattle and come to Ohio. They won't even turn around to look at the camera.

Probably they're the color we'd all choose if we had a choice, but we can't choose. You have to be born that way. To try to duplicate it lying on a beach would be suicide. Most of the rest of the world's people come in ambiguous shades of yellowish tan, reddish yellow, dirt brown, and pinkish gray. Most of us are dissatisfied, and why not?

Those of us belonging to what's politely called the white race find ourselves in springtime the exact shade of newsprint, the background color of the morning paper, without visible signs of life or blood circulation. We take off some of our warm clothes and reveal our flesh, and lo, it's disgusting, and our legs like unto raw clams. To keep from frightening the children, white women need to wear stockings, and nylon is nasty enough in the winter but in summer it's perfectly hateful, clammy, and suffocating.

Once upon a time, we rushed out to do something about it. We anointed ourselves and our friends with oil and cocoa butter and lay spread-eagled upon our towels, courting the changes of sun. The best thing about getting a tan was that it enabled us to spend hours lying around doing absolutely nothing while looking and feeling busy, or at least occupied. We weren't just idly lying there on the warm sand or the green grass letting the sun leach out our winter's bitterness. We were working on our tan. We were gainfully employed.

On Monday when we walked into the office we looked healthy and vigorous, as if we'd spent the weekend on a sailboat. When we looked in the mirror we felt young and strong; our battle scars, our sleepless nights, and our dietary shortcomings had been whisked away by the sunshine fairies. If we were adolescent, pimples, blackheads, and revolting oily or scaly patches had blended into a seamless café au lait. If we were women, we could slip on a pair of sandals and stride into the world barelegged.

The overweight looked suddenly slimmer. The underweight looked less sickly, and indeed, misguided as it now seems, sunlight was once held to be good for us, a source of vitamin D, a painless substitute for cod-liver oil. We could lie in the sun doing nothing because it was for health's as well as beauty's sake.

Sometimes we burned, and young lovers publicly declared their affections by peeling each other's shoulder blades, working delicately, with serious faces.

Those who could afford winter vacations came back to the office in February brown and smug, broadcasting their status more effectively than any postcard; their fellow workers waited spitefully for them to turn yellow in March. Then, in May, even the poorest among us flocked to the parks and beaches and rooftops to seize that finest of all cosmetics, that free unisex blessing, the suntan. Perhaps it did promote wrinkling, as on the many-seamed back of a farmer's neck, but a well-tanned wrinkle looks sturdier than a pale one, more an emblem of the full life lived to the hilt than a mark of impending decay. In the meantime, our teeth looked whiter and our eyes brighter.

From Rio to Stockholm our bodies lay about in public

as fully exposed as possible, in some places entirely exposed, absorbing the glorious rays. In places like London and Seattle, if and when the sun came out the offices emptied and the parks filled with bodies prostrated as for a long-awaited lover.

Now in our more enlightened times, we realize we might as well have been eating ground glass.

In every daily paper, on every weather report, the authorities tell us exactly which grade of sunblock from our extensive wardrobe of sunblocks will protect us this day from a tan. The properly equipped medicine cabinet has room for nothing else; the stuff comes in a range of numbers scientifically calibrated to guard us from December through June and back again. The healthy, once identified by their tans, are now distinguished by corpselike pallor all summer long. Women even show off their legs, all mushroom-colored and stockingless, to signify enlightenment. Not for them the long golden afternoons on a towel in the park; on a sunny day they head for the fluorescent shelter of the shopping mall.

It's the marvel of the earth that the human race has survived, exposed as we were to the sun for millennia, up until the invention of number-30 sunblock along about last Tuesday. And even today there are farmers, trash collectors, landscape gardeners, roofers, park rangers, telephone linemen, sailors, and fishermen who would rather wear tutus than sunblock. Many of them are still alive after decades of this reckless living.

Sometimes we catch sight of them off duty, strolling quite shamelessly down the street, and for a moment we're confused: what can it be that makes them look so delicious, so handsome and strong, so confident and capable? Why do the rest of us suddenly look like a bucketful of drowned worms?

Well, because they're bad and we're good. I suppose virtue is some consolation. And maybe if medical science continues to make great strides in the coming century, we'll see a pill with which we can change our skins at will, Somalian black to English rose to gentian blue. This will improve the view in the offices and on the summer streets. but so did the primitive old suntan, and it was more fun to loll about on sand or grassy park than it is to swallow pills.

STARS

BACK IN THE DAYS WHEN THE DUTIES OF FATHERS were limited and clearly defined—spanking; math homework; telling little girls how pretty they looked; teaching little boys to throw a ball; asking what they learned in school today—one of their duties was to herd the children outside and show them stars. Most fathers could manage the Big Dipper. More scholarly types could find the Little Dipper, Mars, Venus, and sometimes Orion's belt and sword, or at least they said they could: "Look where I'm pointing, just over that big tree" was scant direction in the olden skies crowded with a thousand points of light.

Scout leaders told their charges with every confidence how the North Star would keep them from getting hopelessly lost in the woods. It was cozy to think that when all else failed, the trail was lost, companions had abandoned you, and night had fallen, a star would take your hand and lead you home, as accurately as it led the ancient navigators across uncharted seas: keep the North Star over your shoulder and no harm shall befall you. Unless, of course, staring over your shoulder you walk off a cliff or into a river.

Children were issued mystifying diagrams of the night sky at various seasons, with imagined lines connecting the dots into the most improbable pictures— how could the ancients have seen those specks of light as Cassiopeia's Chair? And what a lot of time the ancients must have spent lying on their backs in the lawn.

According to these same ancients, stars determined our characters. Stars decided whether we'd be a Cancer, modest and home-loving, or an Aries, brash and tactless, or a Capricorn, responsible and sober-minded. They had secret plans for our futures, and knew to the moment when we would find our love or get hit by a truck. Happy people claimed they were born under lucky stars, as now we're born assigned with lucky lottery numbers, and thanked them for good fortune and narrow escapes. If you said the right words to the first star of the evening, you got your wish.

Since we first opened our eyes as humans, we've been expecting something from the heavens—avenging angels, the Antichrist, little green people in saucers, lightning bolts of divine wrath, a mother ship to carry off group suicides. From time to time Greek gods and goddesses turned people into stars and sent them up there, either as reward or punishment, and they're still there. The firmament gave us an extra dimension to wander through at the same time it kept us in our place.

When I was a summer child here on this mountain, sleeping in a refurbished chicken shed, sometimes I went outside at night to pee in the long grass. The stars were enormous, endless, ominous. The night sky was a million times bigger than the day sky because it had vaulted dimensions reaching up forever and ever, while the blue of day was flat. Back then, it was easy to explain the concept of the universe to a child, right up to the inevitable question, "Where does it stop?" and the answer, "It doesn't." We could well believe it, and it wasn't comfortable. It was a cold and windy thought.

Crouching there in the grass on the mountain, I looked anxiously up at the hugeness and the long filmy scarf of the Milky Way, invisible now for many years. "Gravity," I'd whisper reassuringly to myself. "I can't fall. Gravity sticks me to the ground." But I seemed to myself too small and weightless for gravity to bother with, easily sucked up there to wheel helplessly beyond Andromeda forever, hair afloat. That was the great unknown up there. After the Poles and central Africa had been stripped of their mystery, and before nosy NASA had overloaded us with information, the stars were the last playground of the imagination. On the Mars of our minds, anything could happen.

In those days, even to the young, "stars" meant *stars*, not television personalities.

Ironically, along about the time of the space program, when stars were on the evening news, they started to fade out of our nightly lives. They got smaller and dimmer and fewer. The cities got brighter, stayed up later at night, and bulged out into the countryside, trailing a reddish glow of smudge. Almost everywhere we go a city intercepts the stars, and even in the remotest plains pollution veils them and isolated farmhouses blaze with burglar lights on tall poles, the lodestars of humankind. When we finally travel far enough to get a proper view, and marvel, it turns out that the best and the brightest stars are moving at a fairly steady clip toward the nearest airport.

Here on the mountain, on a good winter night I can

20

see stars overhead and behind me, to the west, but toward the east, toward the fast-approaching city, the only thing that shows through the haze is the full moon, so swollen it seems to throb like a wound, and peculiarly orange. I think it used to be white. The stars, when they do appear, look more like a scattering of salt spilled across the murk than the vaulting worlds beyond worlds that frightened me once. What used to be infinity writ plain closes over our heads like the lid of a shoebox.

As the backyard skies darkened, the scientific telescopes strengthened, and spacecraft went forth equipped with cameras. Stargazing, like so many of our former hobbies, is now a private preserve for professionals only. They bring us back information from light-years away. It seems that the Pleiades are not, after all, the seven grieving daughters of Atlas and Pleione, sent up there to console them for the death of their sisters. And it seems that there are even more stars, more universes out there than we'd thought, and they keep making more of themselves.

But somehow, since we can't go outside in the evening anymore and show them to our children, it doesn't seem to matter as much as it did. Besides, our children think stars only show up for the Academy Awards.

IDLENESS

AN ANTHROPOLOGIST RECENTLY BACK FROM BRAZIL reports on the tribe of Suya, a people so backward, so primitive, that they spend three hours a day earning their living by hunting and gathering and the rest of the time

21

dancing and singing songs that they claim to have learned from trees. In the evenings they sit around smoking and telling stories about their ancestors. They seem endlessly good-natured and smile even at anthropologists.

Efforts are being made to civilize them.

In civilized places idleness, once the prerequisite for abstract thought, poetry, religion, philosophy, and falling in love, has become a character flaw. In America we've managed to stamp it out almost completely, and few people under forty can remember a single moment of it, even in earliest childhood. The phrase "spare time" has vanished from the land. Say "idleness" to any well-adjusted American and all he can think of is golf.

When asked how this came to be, most people would say they work long hours, even nights and weekends. If asked why, I suppose they'd say they need the money. They need to buy things. Probably they already have things, but they always need more.

The Suya don't shop. They catch their own food, build their own huts and canoes, and don't drive cars. They make their own clothes, such as they are; for special occasions they strip to the skin and paint each other all over in elaborate traditional designs. This leaves them plenty of time to play in the river and sit waiting for a tree to teach them new songs.

In the past, except for the busiest days of the Industrial Revolution, even civilized people worked only part of the time. Even the most downtrodden medieval peasant never worked more than 150 days a year, refreshed with holidays and seasonal slack times. Records show that the slaves on American cotton plantations enjoyed similar schedules; their work was brutal, but brief.

Through the first half of the twentieth century, our working hours shrank, and much was talked about the four-day week and the leisurely life of the future. Then, around 1970, work started spiraling up again until, by the early '90's, we were logging in an extra month of it every year. We're busy all the time. We're proud of it, too. Proudly we pay five thousand dollars for a watch that's accurate to the minutest fraction of a moment, instead of twelve dollars for a watch that may be casual about entire seconds: our every instant counts. We rush from thing to thing, from sales conference to day care center to airport, with the brain trailing along behind in a tangle, never quite catching up. I don't know just how the human brain moves from one situation to the next, but we may have outstripped it. We may have left it days behind, somewhere in last Tuesday, still deciding between Cheerios and Wheat Chex for breakfast.

Henry David Thoreau was a conceited gasbag, but he did have a point about weighing your possessions against the hours you spent earning the money to buy them. Hard point to make now, though. The happy owner of a new sixty-thousand-dollar car doesn't wonder how else he would have spent the time he spent earning it. What's time for, if not for making money? What's money for, if not to buy things?

For most of the twentieth century it was considered not quite nice to be rich. Not quite respectable. If you'd inherited the lolly, you were a parasite; if you'd made it yourself, you'd been grinding down the workers and wrenching bread from the widow and orphan. The rich were lampooned in *New Yorker* cartoons and represented in the movies by fat men, vain women, and lecherous mustache-twirling landlords evicting the poor working girl. In 1970, driving a secondhand

Volkswagen meant you had more spiritual matters on your mind than grubbing for money; maybe you were a mathematician or a poet or a college professor; certainly you were a good person, tooling along in your modest old car.

Now the secondhand car means you're a worthless boob, lazy, feckless, and a blot on the neighborhood. It means you've been *idle.*

In the '80s, our much-loved president Ronald Reagan marked the turning point with his dictum: "What I want for this country above all else is that it may always be a place where a man can get rich." It was our new dream. Our new land of the free gleaming on the horizon. For most of us, though, it's hard work and uses up the daylight hours.

Still, there are always hours left around the edges, a Sunday morning here, a Tuesday evening there, when all possibilities for making money have been put on hold. These are our hours for idleness and daydreaming. Hours when we belong exclusively to ourselves; when, like Walt Whitman, we can loaf and invite our souls. How did we come to lose those?

Entertainment ate them. The Suya have no television, no tape players in their cars, no computer games, no Internet sex, nothing we would consider entertainment at all. Work stole our days, but entertainment ate everything left over.

At first it was a treat and then gradually, over several decades, it became an addiction. We've forgotten how to live without it for even twenty minutes; it pours into our heads, drowning out the world, from the moment the timer turns on the bedside radio until it turns it off at night. What would happen to us without entertainment? What black hole of boredom would we drop into, never to be seen again; what menacing creatures would creep from the jungles of the mind?

A good deal of our entertainment is now compulsory. In the waiting room at the car dealership, while mechanics are doing unspeakable things to my engine, I can't get more than three feet away from the television set, which seems forever tuned to *Good Morning America,* whatever the time of day. Once, trying to read a magazine, I turned the volume down, and almost immediately the cashier bustled out of her cage and turned it back up again.

In the nursing home I stood by helplessly while an attendant fastened my grandmother into a wheelchair, pushed her out of her room, and parked her firmly, immovably, in front of the television set hung from the ceiling of the recreation hall. Grandmother had never owned a television set or willingly watched one, but the staff felt it would be wicked to leave her musing alone in her room. It was unhealthy, morbid, to sit there unentertained.

She'd been so busy all her life that idleness now must have seemed like a gift from the gods. In her head she was living back in her native Colorado mountains, teaching in one-room schools, riding in sleighs, trout fishing with my handsome young grandfather. In order to stay there she had to keep her eyes shut and her ears covered—fortunately she was growing deaf—and commit the unwholesome sin of doing nothing instead of watching game shows.

Television, like that first cigarette, looked innocent enough in the beginning, and most people turned it on only when there was something they wanted to watch. Intellectuals bragged that they never watched it except for selected highbrow offerings, mostly British, and perhaps a nature special or a classic movie. Then presently threw up their hands and began to watch anything at all, simply because it was there, and flipped on the set as soon as they walked into the room. People now spend three and a half billion hours of every single day that passes over the world looking at a lighted box. The average American watches four and a half hours of television a day *before* he plugs the rented movie into the VCR.

I startled a group of people the other day by referring to "my television set." Everyone else present had one in each room, like the monitors in *1984*.

It metastasized. The VCR entered the home so that we need never miss one program just because we were watching another at the time. Then it turned out to have other uses, and now returning the rented movies has replaced picking up a loaf of bread as the classic errand. Cable television joined in, differing from the regular thing in that it's limitless and has spawned literally hundreds of offerings; if all else fails we can watch people painting their living rooms, people sitting in rowboats, high-pressure systems creeping across a map, congressmen scratching their ears.

New games could be attached to the television, occupying young and old for still more hours. Then the car radio gave birth to the car tape player, the better to drown one's thoughts while commuting. The computer, formerly considered a work tool, burst into the entertainment world. Computer games are a great improvement over television because they feel busier; you can hardly be considered idle while blowing up galaxies. Besides, a person staring into the computer's eye, even if that's a hand of solitaire on the screen, looks and feels more important than a person staring at a jeep Cherokee commercial.

Even the "information highway" that sounded so serious turns out to be entertainment. For every person downloading research materials about igneous rocks or the Khan dynasty, forty are playing games or arguing with pseudonymous strangers. Truly dedicated Web surfers never need to step back into their own skins and live their lives, and never get any sleep at all. Who would settle for boring sleep and amateur dreams with all the exciting alternatives out there?

Our own lives have become a burden to us, even a nuisance. You can hear it in the Monday-morning voices at the office. The reports of personal adventures —shopping, the lawn mowed, a date, a phone call—are delivered in flattened, lusterless tones, without embellishment, but when the talk turns to movies rented and programs watched the voices brighten with energy and fatten with details. Nothing in our own days measures up to the entertainment world, to the Academy Awards and football games, celebrities living, dying, and making love, families in sitcoms and cops and robbers shooting it out. We've become an audience, somewhere in the shadows beyond camera range and in grave danger of vanishing altogether. At least we're not *idle,* though. We don't have time to be idle. On the jogging trail, we wear a Walkman.

I suppose this might explain the scrawniness of our creative product, and why all new novels seem to be the same novel and all new movies remakes or spin-offs or sequels and all new plays revivals. Actually creating something out of nothing called for idleness and lots of it. You can't write the "Ode on a Grecian Urn" when even your bathroom is wired for sound. You can't learn a new song from a tree with a laptop on your lap.

27

The Dalai Lama, spiritual leader of Buddhism, was visiting California, lecturing on inner peace. Someone in the audience spoke up to ask, "What is the quickest way to enlightenment?" and the Dalai Lama wept.

Granted, even creative idleness could be overdone. Wordsworth, patron saint of sloth ("For oft, when on my couch I lie/In vacant or in pensive mood . . ."), would have committed fewer atrocities if he'd watched more television or had even a part-time job bagging groceries. To wit:

I've watched you for a full half-hour,
Self-poised upon that yellow flower;
And, little Butterfly! indeed
I know not if you sleep or feed.

I suppose a person could be forgiven for *writing* those lines, but publishing them oversteps the bounds of decency. And only a lepidopterist is allowed to spend half an hour trying to decide whether a butterfly is eating or merely struck comatose by his presence.

Without all that old-time idleness, all those vacant hours, we'd have much less perfectly awful poetry. But then, we wouldn't have any of the good stuff at all.

POETRY

NOT SO VERY LONG AGO, AT LEAST CONSIDERED IN geologic terms, the *New York Times* ran a regular Sunday feature—maybe it was called "Queries"—for the aid and comfort of persons who couldn't sleep because a line or two of a poem was imbedded in their heads and wouldn't yield its origin. Some other reader always knew, providing relief for the first and self-esteem for the second.

By the time the feature vanished, few people even noticed.

The only people who still read poetry are poets, and they mostly read their own. In all major population centers you'll find a coffeehouse where poets gather to read works expressing their inmost feelings, a free and effortless new form of therapy. For them, a poem is considered good if it enabled the writer to get some gelatinous glob of feeling off his or her chest. I suppose a bad poem would be one whose author retained some shred of personal dignity or even pandered to the reader with felicitous metaphors and images.

Once considered an art form that called for talent, or at least a craft that called for practice, a poem now needs only sincerity. Everyone, we're assured, is a poet. Writing poetry is good for us. It expresses our inmost feelings, which is wholesome. Reading other people's poems is pointless since those aren't our own inmost feelings.

A few professional poets still shelter in academe, where they read their works to helpless undergraduates or small, badly dressed audiences of other poets all fidgeting and silently rehearsing their own upcoming performances. Their product appears from time to time in select magazines. These modern—or perhaps they're postmodern, whatever that means—works often seem to the uninitiated to make no sense at all. You're not allowed to admit this, though. You're supposed to call them "dense" or, at worst, "inaccessible"; there are no "bad" poems. I can't imagine who reads them, or what they get out of them. Perhaps you can take a course on understanding them, perhaps taught by the authors themselves.

Much old-fashioned poetry was horseshit too, but at least we knew what it meant, so we were free to call it horseshit.

It's impossible to explain to anyone who still has his own hair and teeth that poetry was once a pleasure for reader as well as writer. An ordinary, mainstream pleasure for ordinary folk. Gazing back from the end of the century it's hard to believe, but swarms of nonacademic types once crowded into bookstores demanding Tennyson's *Idylls of the King* or Longfellow's *Song of Hiawatha* or Housman's *Shropshire Lad* and made them best-sellers and their authors financially comfortable.

People used to read poetry because they *wanted to*. They *enjoyed* it. They went on long hiking trips supplied with a slim volume of verse, the better to commune with nature and noble minds. They traveled far and wide to listen to recitations of "Paul Revere's Ride," "The Raven," and "The Ballad of East and West." Every schoolboy could stand up and declaim "Casey at the Bat," after his sister did "Barbara Frietchie" and "Li'l Orphan Annie," with appropriate gestures. People swapped improper limericks as if they were lightbulb jokes. They salted their conversation with quotes, which the listener could deftly cap, thus declaring himself cultural kin. They read sentimental stuff and strong men wept; they read patriotic stuff and rushed off to war; they read humorous verse and fell down laughing.

Poetry packed a peculiar excitement and satisfaction that hasn't been replaced. It raised gooseflesh. (Some have maintained that the gooseflesh factor was the litmus test of true poetry, but I'm not sure; I've had my fur rise up from the stirring cadences of some pretty second-rate stuff.) And back in the days when it was as mainstream as any sitcom, most of it was rhythmic, like music, and much of it rhymed. Modern poets feel those were pretty cheap tricks, designed to appeal to the masses, and appeal to the masses they definitely did. They made the stuff easy to memorize. For susceptible people like me, it didn't need to be consciously memorized at all, it simply marched into the head and set up housekeeping. Permanently.

I expect that in my declining years when I no longer recognize my own children I'll still be able to recite, lips barely moving, "Horatius at the Bridge," "The Forsaken Merman," "The Ballad of the Harp-Weaver"—though I never get clear through that one without crying—Henry V's speech before Agincourt, "There was a young man from Saint Paul," and literally hours' worth of Kipling, which was almost impossible *not* to learn "by heart," as it used to be called. Educators tell us that memorization was the root of all evil, but for some of us it was a satisfying skill that left us with a head full of toys.

They've come in handy. They're useful to brighten the monotony on the interstate, pounding on the steering wheel and chanting,

> "Lie there," he cried, "Fell pirate!
> No more, aghast and pale,
> From Ostia's walls the crowd shall mark
> The track of thy destroying bark;
> No more Campania's hinds shall fly
> To woods and caverns when they spy
> Thy *thrice-accursed sail!*"

31

and then spending a happy five miles rummaging for the next line. I don't care how lowbrow rhyme and meter were, they definitely reached down inside and pushed a button.

Verse is indispensable in the dentist's chair, for distraction, a double challenge now that he pipes a radio into my ears while filing my teeth to points or whatever he's doing in there. I set myself something long and concentrate hard:

> Where, risen from a doubtful seat and half- attainted stall,
> The last knight of Europe takes weapons from the wall,
> The last and lingering troubadour to whom the bird has sung
> That once went winging southward when all the world—

"Let me know if you're experiencing any discomfort."

> Christian captives, sick and sunless, all a laboring race repines,
> Like a race in sunken cities, like a nation in the mines—

"Urgh!"
"Did that bother you? Sorry."

> —and in the skies of morning hung
> The stairways of the tallest gods, when tyranny was young.

"Almost finished."

There was bursting of the hatches up and breaking of the holds
And thronging of the thousands up that labored undersea,
White for bliss and blind for sun and stunned for liberty!
Vivat Hispania! Domino Gloria!

"You may rinse now."

At some point back when the twentieth century was young and innovative, rhyme and meter were declared constricting and lower class, mere doggerel, and they were abolished by the loftier sort in favor of free-range imagery. You could still tell it was poetry because the lines didn't run clear to the right-hand margin, breaking off here and there at random, but at this point poetry's broad public base started shrinking toward the vanishing point.

Rhyme survived for a few decades in song, and some of its finest practitioners bloomed among us like gaudy flowers on a dead tree, and Hart rhymed "sequestering" with "pestering," Coward wrote, "because they hope he/Will impale his sola topi/On a tree," and Sondheim danced verbal capers that enchanted the old guard and irritated critics, who thought he was too clever for his own good. Then the Broadway musical collapsed into expensive spectacle and its songs ceased to matter. Meanwhile, the new songs of the new young, insofar as they had words at all, made no effort to rhyme. The young weren't used to rhyme. It may be one of those windows in the growing mind that seal shut if not opened early. Parents no longer have time to read nursery rhymes and children no longer hang out

33

together unsupervised, teaching each other to chant "I see England, I see France, I see Susan's underpants," which led on to "You'll wonder where the yellow went/When you brush your teeth with Pepsodent," paving the way for "In Xanadu did Kubla Khan . . ." The advertising jingle, once imprinted on the growing mind, vanished as the new verse-deaf young moved into the creative departments.

Rhyme had given us pleasure for centuries. Prayers rhymed: "Now I lay me down to sleep, I pray the Lord my soul to keep." Among a largely illiterate population, useful information was handed down in verse, lest we forget: "An apple a day keeps the doctor away;" "Sow peas and beans in the wane of the moon/Who soweth them sooner, he soweth too soon;" "Berries red, have no dread; Berries white, poisonous sight." Weather forecasts rhymed: "When the dew is on the grass/Rain will never come to pass." Incantations rhymed: "Star light, star bright, first star I've seen tonight . . ." Children learned to read in verse: "In Adam's fall/We sinned all."

Rhyme touched some receptor in the head, now atrophied. It satisfied. It tied a knot in the thought. In spite of the modern insistence that only content counts and form is somehow dishonest, "All I could see from where I stood/Was three long mountains and a wood" is different from "All I could see from where I was standing/Was three long mountains and a wood."

Generations raised on the flat-footed, colorless voice of television instead of the mysteries of Mother Goose regard anything called poetry, rhymed or not, with darkest suspicion. If it isn't personal therapy, then it's a timewasting complication of the facts. It uses metaphor and simile, which the young consider flimflam and

34

struggle to translate into what the poet is "really" saying, or would have said if he'd had any sense: "The fog comes on little cat feet" *simply isn't true,* and if he means "quietly," why not just say so?

For 450 years the King James version of the Bible alerted even the illiterate to the joyous possibilities of language. Now it's under fire from all sides. Too confusing, too inaccessible, too flowery. The Word needs no cosmetics, none of your slippery poet's tricks. Language is a means to an end; making it a pleasure in itself is decadent. Information rules. New, improved; demystified Bibles spring up on all sides.

In the bad old version, the Twenty-third Psalm declared, "Yea, though I walk through the valley of the shadow of death, I will fear no evil," and that, boys and girls, is poetry; observe the gooseflesh on the forearms.

In the Revised English version, we get

Even were I to walk through a valley of deepest darkness
I should fear no harm, for you are with me;
Your shepherd's staff and crook afford me comfort.

(Pity the preacher; imagine declaiming that in sonorous, ringing tones from the pulpit.) The valley of the shadow was a metaphorical place, the valley in the mind where dread dwells and nameless evil stalks. The valley of deepest darkness is only a valley, and the harm is probably stubbing our toe on a real rock, having forgotten our real flashlight. And note the brave, nose-thumbing "will" replaced by the limp gray subjunctive; have these people no ears?

Apparently not. Nor do they miss them. Quite the contrary; at the mention of poetry, most people now look uncomfortable and change the subject, as if it had been a particularly dotty and embarrassing relative whose death has come as a relief to all.

It's odd how quickly it happened, this tectonic shift that extracted a whole dimension from our lives. It was one of our very oldest pleasures, maybe almost as old as speech itself. It was how we kept the chronicle of our past, and we huddled together by firelight to listen to epics that took all night in the telling, and went away refreshed. Then it was written down. It accumulated, and filled whole libraries. It immortalized landmark occasions, melted the maiden's heart, emboldened the timid, inspired the young, and comforted the old.

Then, in the space of a single lifetime, it vanished. Strange are the paths of progress.

TAVERNS

THE PERENNIAL COMIC STRIP "ANDY CAPP" HAS recently been banished from the *Washington Post* as an evil influence, and small wonder. In Andy's world there are only three scene changes—his pub, his living room, and the street in between. Sometimes he tries to entice a lass at the bar. Sometimes he brings his wife, to swap acid comments with the bartender. Sometimes she awaits him at home, in curlers, with a rolling pin. The story line has a mythic simplicity, the endlessly repeated escapes to conviviality and returns to domesticity, Huck's world and Aunt Polly's forever at cross-purposes.

Andy's English, so he gets away with it. If he were American, he'd be guilty of abusing beer and punished with professional counseling. Five or ten years ago, the

36

authorities in charge of our health were saying that a couple of drinks a day were actually good for us, and fortified the heart in the medical as well as the emotional sense. Now they've changed their minds, as they often do. Having finished establishing tobacco as the Grim Reaper and assuring the populace that those who resist it will live, if not forever, at least for a thousand years, they found themselves with no rousing battle to fight, reduced to nattering about fruits and vegetables. They dropped from the headlines and the top of the news hour. Desperate, they pounced on what they call "alcohol." ("A round of alcohol for the bar, Pete, and have one yourself.") Alcohol is our new killer. Even small amounts of alcohol. Even the civilizing glass of wine and the cold beer of a summer's afternoon are as poisonous as warm gin from the bottle.

Millions believe them. But then, millions have been believing them for decades, faithfully trotting after their twists and turns. Millions even ate oat bran, a harmless abrasive substance derived from boot scrapers, when told to do so.

Americans, when not at work or out jogging, are supposed to stay home embracing family values, each encased in his separate walls, and drink bottled water. The neighborhood tavern languishes. After it closes down, it reopens as a coffee shop, virtuous tavern-substitute of the century's end.

Coffee shops are not the same. As a devoted fan of canned Maxwell House, I don't frequent them willingly, but I've been dragged in by up-to-date friends who claim they can distinguish among a dozen Colombian blends and sniff out Ethiopian Yirgacheffe at twenty paces. In a coffee shop there are tables where people sit drinking coffee and avoiding eye contact with neighboring tables.

Sometimes there's a counter where people hunch over their caffeine facing, not a friendly barkeep and rows of gleaming bottles, but a blank wall or a window onto traffic. For unknown reasons, it would be as invasive to open conversation with one's neighbor here as it would be at a lunch counter. A counter is not a bar.

The company of one's fellow creatures was always the point of the public house. Samuel Johnson said the pub was the throne of human felicity; E. B. White praised the "golden companionship of the tavern." The American decline in public quaffing raises the disturbing question of why we no longer seek out golden companionship except in the sanitized, faceless privacy of the Internet.

Historically the tavern's enemies always ignored its social joys and claimed it was merely a place to get drunk, an evil snare wherein the once-decent family man destroyed his health and drank up his loved ones' grocery money. But humans are nothing if not ingenious and when they wanted to get pie-eyed they never really needed a tavern. Fermenting and distilling are simple processes by which bulky crops like apples, corn, and potatoes could be much reduced in bulk, though not in value, and sold locally in barrels or jugs instead of hauled to market in a cart. Before freezers, before Mason jars, an oversupply of perishables could thus be preserved indefinitely; a lady diarist traveling through my own area of Virginia in 1755 was refreshed en route with "peach whiskey."

The making of drinkable wine, ale, and beer was more laborious, a job for professionals. For these, the citizen traditionally repaired to bistro, trattoria, *biergarten,* taverna, or corner pub to drink in company, perhaps to sing, play darts or backgammon, and hear the news. Not Dan Rather's news but the important news—whose crops had been flattened by hail, who got married, who got mugged, who got fired, and how the man on the next barstool finally had his old cat put down and can't stop grieving.

Don't we care anymore?

In the countryside, where the "ordinary house" was often the second or third building constructed in a newly forming town, it was blessed as a place to see people instead of cows and chickens, and functioned as a clearinghouse of information on swine fever, horse races, and grain prices. In the bygone days of slow travel, taverns along the roads provided sleeping quarters for man and horse, and here the local folks went to hear news from the passerby, from beyond the mountain, across the river; to see a gloriously unfamiliar face and pick up new tales to tell. And always, in cities, the corner tappie made a familiar safety zone in the chaos and introduced neighbors who would never otherwise meet.

Behind the swinging doors in the wild old West, land of bachelors, the saloon in Sagebrush City provided the only available social life. Here, according to the movies, deals were made, scores were settled, no-good women danced on the bars, folks with aces concealed in their clothing were shot dead, and from time to time splendid brawls broke out, rich with crashing bottles, splintering mirrors, and brandished barstools. In short, everything to brighten the mind with memories during the lonely months on the range or the homestead or, perhaps, in jail.

With Prohibition the American tavern went underground, became a speakeasy, and partook of some of the western tradition, the spice of police raids and gangster shootouts flavoring the bootleg hootch. After Prohibition's repeal, the tavern lost its drama but regained its dignity as a haven—anchor of neighborhoods and center of civic and political life.

Perhaps, in hindsight, the end began back in the early 1950s when television sets appeared behind the bar. They seemed like a good idea at the time. They were rare in homes—many sensible people didn't even *want* them in their homes—but from time to time events appeared on them and extra customers flocked into the bar to watch a heavyweight bout or an election. This rejoiced the hearts of the management while secretly undermining its future.

Television is noisy. It makes casual conversation an effort and confiding in bartenders too loud to be confidential. Even with the sound turned off, television is distracting. Images squirm around on the screen. A row of people at a bar, confronted by television, tend to ignore each other and stare at the set. The whole purpose of the tavern fades: why be here at all?

One by one the customers bought their own televisions and realized that, without fellowship, there wasn't much point in the pub, and they might as well save the money, buy a six-pack, and sit home with their shoes off. There they still sit.

In the '70s, the Age of Sex, watering holes enjoyed a renaissance, and people called "singles" went to places called "singles bars" in search of love. This was not the tavern-as-haven that we knew for millennia but more like the tavern as shopping center; "golden companionship" took on a different meaning. Then sex as a hobby crashed almost overnight and the '70s were replaced by the '80s, by health and fitness and the solitary joys of jogging and carrot juice that still haunt us today. The bar was condemned anew as a den of iniquity, black with the sins of alcohol and secondhand smoke.

At the dawn of the current decade I lived in the middle of a city and rejoiced in a neighborhood tavern around the corner, fallen on shabby days but still in business. The television was consigned to the far end, beyond the bar, and anyone determined to turn it on had to retreat back there to the rickety table underneath it. Except in times of national emergency nobody did.

To this tavern repaired a goodly handful of local residents on our evening routes between work and apartment. We had little in common except this destination, but we accepted each other without question. The bar is the essence of democracy, the great leveler, literally as well as figuratively.

At a bar, everyone is the same size. Elsewhere some men are taller than others and the discrepancy is of great concern to them, odd as this seems to women. Standing at a cocktail party, men must struggle with the responsibilities of tallness or the humiliations of shortness; you can watch it from a distance in their postures and the pitch of their voices. Because height is largely a matter of lens, on barstools they finally see eye to eye, equals.

Over a period of several years we at the tavern grew to know each other as well as we knew our immediate families. We knew the names of each other's bosses, landlords, dogs, siblings. Hand in hand we passed through stormy love affairs, a painful coming-out, career changes, surgery. When Steve's divorce was final he bought drinks for the bar. When I had a new book out, so did I. Except for the chance street encounter we never saw each other elsewhere, and this gave our friendships a luminous, self-contained quality, limiting responsibility, enhancing pleasure. Unless you count James, who wintered outside on the steam vent and joined us only when driven by thirst, we weren't sad, mad loners; we all had jobs, families, social lives. But we had this separate place too, this undemanding refuge that was neither here nor there.

The barkeeps, though moody, were always interesting people, hand picked by the owner for compatibility rather than "mixology"; indeed, they flatly refused any assignment more taxing than a martini, which drove away suburbanites and the trendy.

The perfect neighborhood tavern.

On a Saturday afternoon my sister called me at home to say that our mother had died, quite unexpectedly. I sat for a long time staring at the telephone, wondering what to do next. A dozen phone calls had to be made. Sympathy must be extended and received. Responsibilities shouldered. My office alerted, a suitcase packed, a train caught. Deep in shock, I wasn't ready for any of this.

I put on my coat and walked around the corner.

It was early and the bar was empty except for the bartender, and he was a substitute. A stranger. I'd never seen him before. Still he was a bartender, one of the last of the dwindling breed of comforters, trusted instinctively. I sat down at the end.

"What can I do for you?" he asked.

I couldn't remember what I usually drank. "I don't know," I said stupidly. "My mother just died."

He turned on his heel and walked up the length of the bar to the trap door, came out and down the row of bar-stools to mine. Silently he gave me an enormous, hard, smothering hug, then went back behind the bar and poured me a double whiskey on the house, set it in front of me, and left me alone with it. Up at the far end he stood dunking glasses, silent but available.

I nursed my drink. Confusion smothered my mind and all I knew, the one fact I could grasp, was that I was in the right place. The only right place. Not yet surrounded by family and friends, not still alone in my apartment staring at the telephone, but here on this barstool.

The last time I visited the city, the tavern was closed and the building was for sale.

Where will the regulars go when their mothers die?

PICNICS

IN SOME STATES, AS YOU'RE SPEEDING ALONG THE major highways you pass a sign with a picture of a picnic table and a tree. Just beyond it, you pass the table itself, set safely back from the highway's verge, tethered next to a tethered trash can. Nobody has ever been seen sitting there, but it's touching to think of the bureaucrats who arranged for it, the planners from the highway department, perhaps in conference with planners from Parks and Recreation, prepared to lay out money on clearing the space, installing the table with its benches attached, and maybe, should the need arise, emptying the trash can of paper plates and soda cans.

How old can they be, these sentimental executives, that they have such tender memories of eating under a tree? In their mind's eye they can see the happy family beside their car, the white cloth laid over the splintery boards, the wicker basket opened, the cold chicken and potato salad handed out, the thermos of lemonade, the hot winds of exhaust fumes rustling the paper napkins, and everyone shouting happily to each other through the roar of trucks as if it were the ocean's roar. They remember picnics, these busy men in suits, and in a burst of kindliness they arrange for us, the travelers, to have such memories too.

There are no takers. Tree or no tree, the driver with hamburger in lap, drink in the drinks-holder, is not inspired to disable his cruise control and pause in his headlong flight through space. Who has time? Our weekends are frantic with errands, and the warm-weather holidays that once cried out for picnics now demand to be spent at the shopping mall, abloom with celebratory bargains not to be missed.

Twenty years ago, in the springtime, the banks of the Schuylkill River in Philadelphia flowered for miles with families lunching on the grass, like an endless French painting unscrolling around the river bends. All the innercity picnickers were dressed as if for a party, fresh in their springtime colors and prints, punctuated here and there with puffs of barbecue smoke. Now joggers and runners, scowling, pound back and forth on the grassy banks and the lunchers are gone. The picnic's day is done.

As a form of recreation, eating under a tree seems pretty flaccid now, compared with our exciting options. As a novelty, it's nowhere. Once upon a time packing a meal and eating it somewhere far from the dinner table was a charming anarchy, a relief from the endless repetition of Papa at the head of the table, the fork laid out on a folded napkin to the left of the plate, knife and spoon to the right, salt and pepper and family members all in their accustomed places. Now every meal is a picnic. At different times, depending on their schedules, those who haven't grabbed something on their way home scatter throughout the house with a slice of pizza to dine informally in front of the computer or the television set. Anarchy is routine; for novelty, once or twice a year they sit at the dinner table with a fork on a folded napkin to the left.

In the suburban summers the barbecue grill lays its sweet smoke across the neighborhood from decks and patios. Here, feeling primitive, the man of the house cooks meat, but the patio is plagued by wasps at lunchtime and mosquitoes in the evening, by the rumble of traffic and the snarl of weed-eaters, and there's not much to do out there. The family takes its cooked meat and retreats into the air-conditioning and its electronic pleasures.

In the olden days, before home entertainment, people longed to get away for what they called "a change of scene." They piled into carriage or car or trolley and went elsewhere, and when they arrived at the city park, the ocean, the lake, the river, Stonehenge, Gettysburg, the cliffs, the ruins, or—according to many humorous accounts—the field concealing a raging, unsuspected bull, no franchise there sold ready-cooked food. Bizarre as it now seems, people had to bring their own.

The working man's family packed beer and ham sandwiches and the lord of the manor's brought smoked salmon, watercress sandwiches, and champagne, with staff to carry the baskets. (One manners manual of the mid-nineteenth century warns against taking more than two or three servants, on pain of looking ridiculous, and besides, "half the fun is lost if the gentlemen do not officiate as amateur waiters.") They spread it forth and had a picnic, telling each other that everything tastes better outdoors.

The word *picnic* seems to have come from the French *pique-niqne* and originally meant potluck; a meal, indoors or out, to which each guest contributed. Early in the nineteenth century it took on its present meaning, but there were picnics in plenty before they had a name. A hundred and fifty years before the word appeared, the London diarist Samuel Pepys and his merry companions were carrying food and a deck of cards to parks and grassy hillsides. Long before that, according to the painters, gods and goddesses picnicked on the slopes of Olympus, naked among bowls of wine and fat, lolling bunches of grapes. In the Old Testament the Lord himself laid a picnic table in the green pastures, beside the still waters.

Customs, however ancient, get supplanted and wither. Like whistling in the streets, the loss of picnics is less sad in itself than the loss of the impulse behind it; not that the picnic, with its accompanying ants and thunderstorms, has disappeared, but that we no longer want it, no longer care to spread a cloth at the cliff's edge and eat and drink together and throw our crumbs to the seagulls; no longer even pull off the highway to the table provided by bureaucrats.

We still have "family picnic areas" attached to amusement parks, acknowledging that modern children would he bored to madness with nothing but Nature to play with; here they can swallow some food before scampering off to the Tilt-A-Whirl. A whiff of cynicism mingles with the smell of popcorn oil: we are here because the proprietors want to make money from our presence, and they do. They charged admission, probably sold us food, and the Tilt-A-Whirl costs extra. The innocence is gone.

Near civilized cities, box lunches are available for purchase at outdoor concerts, to be eaten on the grass, but this seems suspiciously sophisticated, these urbane music lovers pretending to have an old-time picnic, like Marie Antoinette playing shepherdess. Besides, though they wouldn't be caught dead at an amusement park, these people too have paid admission and expect to be entertained as well as fed.

In other areas, the annual company picnic yet survives, another un-innocent occasion. The corporate organizers in their paternal wisdom arrange an outing designed to keep the employees grateful and docile for almost no outlay at all. It takes place outside of company time, so no man-hours are lost. The field and the tables are cheap or free, and where else can you feed a grown man a charred hotdog on a cold bun and call it lunch? Softball afterwards, with borrowed bat and ball, costs them nothing and promotes the team spirit and loyalty so essential to obedient hired help. Attendance is more or less compulsory. Nobody tells Corporate how the employees hate it, or how their spouses and children have been known to break their own legs to get out of going.

Less cynical but no more fun is the food-as-fuel picnic that goes with strenuous activity. These meals are designed for portability; no bulky salmon mousse or heavy champagne bottles; just seeds, raisins, and packets of dust and flakes to mix with water. The resulting energy will enable the picnicker to finish scaling the mountain or climbing back to the trailhead. The English traditionally carry chocolate for the same purpose, but Americans believe that anything so palatable would defeat the purpose; suffering is a prerequisite of virtue. Virtue, or the defeat of sin through sweat and toil, has replaced innocence, the effortless absence of sin.

Nobody toiled at the picnic of yore. Sometimes they brought a croquet set. Sometimes someone brought a cornet or a fiddle; sometimes they sang. Young persons of opposite sexes could take a lighthearted stroll beyond the eye of chaperones. There was fishing or swimming, sketching and watercolors, excursions into the cave or through the ruins. Children played tag or hide-and-seek, fell in the lake, teased the cows, dared each other to climb trees or rocks, caught butterflies, fireflies, toads, newts, and beetles, some of which they put down their sisters' backs, or took off their shoes and caught minnows in the creek with empty paper cups.

Before the invention of the portable grill, food was assembled at home and expected to be cold at the picnic. Sometimes the cole slaw spoiled in the sunshine and poisoned the picnickers. Sometimes, daringly, dry ice was packed with it and the car windows kept open so the gasses could escape. A cold creek or spring in which to float the food could save your life.

Certain foods came to be sacred to picnics, like deviled eggs, rarely served indoors and, being fragile and slippery, always a challenge to transport safely. Eggs were hard-boiled, cooled, and carefully sliced in half lengthwise. The yolks were popped out, mashed up with mustard, mayonnaise, and creative touches like chopped pickles or Worcestershire sauce, and replaced in the whites. Dedicated picnic packers stuffed the yolk mixture into fluted pastry tubes so it came out in curlicues. The final touch was a sprinkling of paprika, a red cosmetic powder widely used to brighten colorless foods. Then they were packed prayerfully into a straight-sided dish so they wouldn't slither en route.

They were eaten in the hand, messily. For the respectable middle class accustomed to more than one fork at meals, half the joy of the picnic was eating with their fingers. They tore apart cold chicken and barbecued spareribs and chewed the bones; they picked up the strawberries by the tasseled end. (Strawberry season was excuse enough for a picnic, since at home decency required them to be sliced and sugared and eaten with spoons.) Picnickers plunged their faces into watermelon and broke off chunks of cake. Peach juices dribbled down their chins. Bones and apple cores were winged into the bushes. Probably they talked with their mouths full. It was a glad cathartic orgy of unthinkable manners, sanctified by the outdoors.

My grandparents, long ago in Colorado, often climbed the hills to a likely-looking stream and built a fire, buried potatoes in the coals, heated the skillet and then, when it was hot, caught and gutted a trout to throw in it fresh and sizzling. I don't know what they did afterwards. Grandmother didn't tell me, but they were very young and whatever they did. I'm sure innocence lay over it like sunlight.

Innocence was an essential ingredient in picnics. Picnics provided a temporary rebirth into a sinless state; wherever we spread our blanket and opened our basket was a pre-apple Eden. In novels, even the villain turns out to be human in the open air, sandwich in hand. In all those Impressionist picnic paintings, clothing could be doffed without prurience; indoor nakedness was suggestive, nakedness on the grass was a celebration. Where lunch was spread out under the sky, sin hadn't yet uncoiled its head.

An enthusiasm for picnics required a belief in the possibility of innocence. We may have stopped believing.

OLD THINGS

MY LITTLE BROTHER NICK WAS A HANDFUL, OR WHAT was called at the time a problem child. Five years older, I kept trying to interpret him to our elders, but he was hard to explain. Among his other quirks, he was afraid of new possessions. He backed away scowling from the department-store bag borne in through the front door: something would be lurking in it to replace something he loved.

Like all proper little boys, he wore bib overalls winter and summer. Our mother was working as a display artist in a department store at the time and consequently, though clothes bored her, for that brief period in our lives new clothes came home. Nick came to anticipate them, suspiciously, sniffing them out as Mother approached the front door. Sometimes he was right. His overalls, outgrown and worn colorless at the knees, were under sentence of death and new overalls, identical except for being whole and larger, barged into the front hall.

Like a cat, Nick knew what was in the bag before it was opened. He backed away. "Just wear my old ovryalls," he whispered. Mother flourished the new ones, infinitely superior, in full bloom of their blueness and wholeness of knee, and praised their superiority. Nick backed clear up against the wall. "Old ovryalls," he explained. His clothes, having been worn, were his. His spirit had soaked into them and they were flesh of his flesh. His soul was in them, and theirs in his. They were comfort, they were known, as the Indians knew their ancestral hills. The new ones smelled of sizing and stood stiffly in the air, with neither soul nor comfort. To wear them would be to bed down among strangers and go forth friendless to nursery school.

Lines were drawn in the sand. Ultimatums were issued. Nick was forced to resort to a full-blown tantrum, for which he was spanked and sent to bed supperless, as children were in those days. I tried to explain his position and was sent in turn to my room.

In the end, of course, the grown-ups won. Life is a casting off. Even with such unworldly parents we couldn't always wear our old clothes, sleep on our sagging mattresses under our ratty blankets, travel in our accustomed car, or live all our lives in our accustomed house.

Not that we didn't try, all of us. Mother, a writer of children's books, clung to the end to her ancient portable manual typewriter. At Christmas, when we grew old enough to offer Christmas presents, her children regularly suggested the gift of something more advanced, and regularly she rejected us with cries of outrage. It was a hateful typewriter, even by the standards of its breed and time. Almost weightless, it leapt onto the floor when you slammed the carriage across too fast. The S and the U stuck. At speeds of over twenty words a minute all the keys fused and had to be untangled by hand. The space bar skipped. The backspace key worked only sometimes, and the keyboard was so cramped your fingers got wedged in it so the whole nasty little machine clung to you and had to be shaken off like a crab. It was hers, though. True ownership of anything requires time, and Mother and the typewriter had been together for decades; she knew the sort of things it wrote, and there was no telling what peculiar prose a new one might produce. *Finnegans Wake?* Pornography? Minimalism? The old one, chattering and sidling across the desk, churned out withering letters to the editor until Mother's death, when her children dumped it vengefully in the trash.

My brother Nick grew up to be prosperous and much respected in his field, and he wears his shirts until they dangle from his collarbone in tatters and drives his cars to the brink of the graveyard, lulled by their familiar squeaks and smells and character flaws, the hacking cough on a winter's morning, the resistance to second gear, the shimmy at fifty-two miles an hour.

Luckily he's successful enough to be considered merely eccentric instead of miserly or, worse, poor.

In America's most recent years, personal prosperity has come to be the measure of our worth as human beings, and new things are the flag prosperity flies. Schoolchildren have been known to murder one another for the latest footwear. Yesterday's purchase is as dross and ashes to us; today's is overshadowed by the prospect of tomorrow's. We mark our progress through life possession by possession, casting off the old almost before we've learned its name and celebrating our patriotic and religious holidays at shopping malls, harvesting fresh goods to replace the stale. This year's computer is but a temporary substitute for next year's. Even the new house, even as we unlock its door and step inside to the smell of new paint and new carpeting, is haunted by anticipation of the next new house, with even larger rooms and fresher paint.

The landfills bulge with yesterday's new computers. New houses sprout from every cornfield, and secondhand houses stand abandoned all down last year's streets, For Sale signs weathering and fading, the height marks of growing children still visible on the bathroom doorjambs, cigarette burn on windowsill, and, between the living room floorboards, pine needles from a Christmas tree.

We came to this wholesale abandonment only yesterday. Generations gone before us, even recently before us, remembering the lean years of the Great Depression and then the scarcities of the war years, believed in keeping things. For them, endurance was a virtue; quality *meant* durability. Things were supposed to "last," an alien concept now.

My grandmother mended things. In her hands the broken plate was made whole again, and when sheets wore thin in the center she ripped them down the middle and sewed them together edge to edge for another five years' service. She darned the holes in the heels and toes of socks. She let out the seams and dropped the hems of my outgrown clothes, which had been chosen originally for their ample seams and hems. She wasn't poor; it was just that in her generation it was slatternly to throw away that which could be rescued.

Mending things once supported a many-branched industry of professions. Even quite ordinary furniture was sanded and refinished and its wobbly legs braced and shimmed. Shoe soles and heels were replaced, over and over. Patches were applied to flat tires, trouser knees and jacket elbows, and, in the days of traveling tinkers, pots and pans. The coils of the butt-sprung couch were retied and fresh padding and fabric laid on. Chairs were recaned and lamps rewired and silver replated and scissors reground until over the years the contents of the family home grew a soulful patina of resurrections and rebirths. The well-worn state of the everyday brightened the status of the Sunday best; the new bonnet; the real china, brittle and translucent, for honoring guests; the polished front parlor reserved for brides, corpses, the

53

preacher, and the Christmas tree.

In the attic there were trunks. You can still find trunks for sale, but they're sold as coffee tables. Nobody now keeps the stuff that once lived in trunks and cartons in attics, the theater programs, shawls, fans, school report cards, still-bright stacks of *National Geographics,* tarnished jewelry, Mason jars, christening gowns, medals, diaries, certificates, souvenir postcards, seashells, children's drawings, scrapbooks stuffed with valentines and newspaper clippings, and the pink satin shoes in which some vanished great-aunt once danced till dawn.

Who needs it? It's old. Besides, in a couple of years we'll be buying a newer house, and think of the nuisance of moving it all.

Much of what we live with is made of materials that don't age; they just go on and on until they break or obsolesce or we get bored with them. An unspoken, inadmissible reason Americans go to Europe is to look at old things. Not just old paintings, but shabby things, bleached-out, worn-down things, stone steps with their centers hollowed by feet and thatched roofs sagging under the years; a gatepost gnawed and pocked by weather. We don't know why we want to look at them. We just do.

The United States government, in figuring our gross national product, defines "durable goods" as anything that will last three years.

Recently friends of mine built a second house, far away in the mountains, and I went to visit them there. The place was a hymn to prosperity, a pinnacle of achievement. It was big and sunny and everything in it was new. Not just the walls and roof, not just the furniture, but the plates and cups and glasses, the sheets and towels and the cake of soap in the bathroom and the shrubbery in the garden. Even the books were new. The antiques were new, freshly bought from experts, not something from the family attic. Nothing was shabby, or even dusty, as if we had dropped here nameless onto a new-made planet without footprints, where no comfortable message had been left behind in a bottle.

I slept badly, with anxious dreams, and kept waking up, in the new bed, under the new quilt. It was like trying to sleep in a store.

I thought of my mother's living room, its Oriental rug worn down to gray where the feet were most frequent. Less domestic than Grandmother, Mother still felt there was something vulgar about replacing anything just because it was old. The bookcases were crammed with sets of Kipling and Dickens and Mark Twain, bindings cracked and taped. The outlines of an armchair could be seen through the ghost of an uncle reading the evening paper. The heavy linen curtains were bleached in long streaks from the sun and held the echo of their curtain rings' rattle as they were drawn against eight thousand twilights and opened on eight thousand mornings, while inside the children grew taller and the parents' hair turned gray and then white.

In my friend's new house in the mountains I turned on the new lamp on the new bedside table, for comfort in the unpeopled night, and remembered Nick's old overalls. I even thought kindly, for a moment, of Mother's typewriter. Its spirit was recalcitrant and its soul was a cranky one, but at least it had grown a soul. It takes time to grow soul. It takes time for our homes and possessions to gather fingerprints enough to keep us company.

Perhaps, in twenty years, or fifty, I'll go back to the mountain house and sleep with better dreams. By then the switch on the bedside lamp will have developed character flaws, and need jiggling.

PIANOS

I CAN'T FIGURE OUT WHERE THEY ALL WENT, THE pianos, or an how they disappeared so quickly. There were millions of them, just yesterday, and they were big, and wouldn't rot away easily into compost. The intricate construction inside them was made of brass and heavy wires, as every child knew from lifting the lid and striking a key and watching the hammer hit home, producing a note. Then the child could step on the sustaining pedal and try it again, and the house quivered to the long sound until the child's mother said, "You can either practice or come out in the kitchen and help me peel potatoes, one or the other." The piano's inside was full of indestructible stuff and the outside was varnished to a fare-thee-well, so even years of rain in the landfill wouldn't reduce the whole structure to mush. Yet suddenly they were gone. Somewhere out there lies a wasteland the size of Nebraska piled thirty feet high with spinets and baby grands, summer suns and winter frosts peeling their veneer off in curls and loosening the ivory of keys and snapping wires that lash out at the deaf air with one last, long, despairing B flat. Sprinkled among them are the piano stools, their round tops covered in plush, upon which a small child could twirl until his head spun, and the piano benches broad enough for duets, whose lids lifted up to reveal sheet music for "Clementine" and "O Susanna." And somewhere underneath them all lie the bones of those who tended them, the itinerant piano tuners; the proud

56

piano movers, so superior to those who moved mere beds and tables; and the proprietors of elegant stores that sold nothing but pianos and perhaps a parlor organ, employing a man to entice customers by playing sweetly on the merchandise.

Once pianos lived among us. In the novels of Jane Austen the reader is rarely out of sight of a pianoforte. Whenever the situation gets tense or the guests grow mopey, one of the womenfolk is asked to play. How she accepts the invitation is an important guide to character. She shouldn't blush and squirm and need urging, but rise at once and comply, smiling, with neither undue modesty nor undue pride. Deportment counts more than talent, and many a heart is smitten by her sweetness and grace at the keyboard. She should play a couple of songs and desist, unless pressed for a third; not, like the odious Mary in *Pride and Prejudice,* flaunt her whole repertoire while the company fidgets.

In America, the piano was basic to respectability and no family could rise from working class to middle class or from rustic to civilized except they were accompanied by a piano. We even took them west. Anyone who has tried to move a piano from one side of the room to another will appreciate the nuisance they were in a covered wagon that had to be unloaded for river crossings and its contents ferried across and then reloaded. Pigheadedly, though, we clung to them. If the load had to be lightened, we might throw out the cookstove first. It wasn't the only music; someone in every group had brought a fiddle, but a fiddle is footloose, a gypsy instrument disconnected from home, propriety, and domestic virtue. The piano meant that even though we had said good-bye to the amenities of home and friends and plunged toward our destiny of utter desolation surrounded by savages, we should not sink to savage state ourselves. Even though our new home might be a one-room log cabin with snow blowing in through the chinks, there would be music in it; we would still be ladies and gentlemen at heart, and appreciate the finer things in life, and our children would not grow up barbarians.

East and west across the country, as late as the 1970s, children were given piano lessons. Almost as important as clean clothes, they were the mark of responsible parents and worth scrimping and sacrificing to pay for. After school every proper household echoed to the sound of scales and "Clair de Lune." The verb *to practice* now usually involves soccer, but to those who came before it meant "The Happy Farmer." "I can't, I have to practice," said every well-brought-up Dick and Jane, and their pianoless friends slunk away, social status trailing in the dust.

For a significant slice of the population, teaching piano was the only acceptable way for a married woman to supplement the family income: she could do it at home. To step out from under the sheltering roof and earn money in public would have brought shame on her husband, but receiving urchins in her own parlor and placing their wobbly fingers on the keyboard was both private and cultural. To this end, piano lessons for little girls were essential vocational training and the only hedge against future want. For boys, they would be a useful social tool.

Parties happened more easily and more often in the olden days; a piano and three or more people constituted a party. The young man who had sacrificed some of his childhood afternoons pounding the keyboard could now sight-read or play by ear a wide range of songs that, until recently, everyone in the room knew. That young man was much in demand and, like Jane Austen's heroines, the center of flattering attention. He played "Sweet Betsy from Pike" and "Swannee River" and everyone sang, and the happiness came not from the quality of the music, rarely high, but the joy of fellow-feeling: we were all singing the same words. Rugs were rolled up and pitched into the hall, tables and chairs pushed against the walls, and dancing broke out. Later, more sophisticated, we all knew the Broadway songs and the young man played "Mountain Greenery" and "My Funny Valentine" and everyone still knew the words.

We sang without shame, because the competition was less intense then. When sound reproduction was young, the phonograph produced a scratchy, faint facsimile of music beside which Uncle Bill sounded just as good as Enrico Caruso and much easier to understand.

The piano player was in demand beyond the parlor, too. Pianos were required furniture in drinking establishments. Expensive places hired a professional, dressed in tails, to play soft romantic arrangements during cocktail hour, but in the corner tavern the piano was up for grabs. The young man could float from pub to pub and never pay for his own beer, playing "When Irish Eyes Are Smiling" while the denizens yodeled mournfully and then sent him another beer and called out requests.

It was during the great American watershed years of the late 1960s that music began to shift under our feet. The same respectability that had made the piano a middle-class shrine now made it look stodgy and hide-bound. While Junior was still practicing scales, his older sister was ironing her hair and playing antiwar folk songs on a guitar; if she remembered the words to "Surrey with the Fringe on Top," she would have died rather than admit it.

Halfway through the '70s it was clear that rock 'n' roll wasn't about to go away, and it was antipiano. Like the fiddlers on the western journey, it was footloose stuff, irresponsible by design, and it needed volume, not pianos. Imagine the Beatles dragging one around. Ragtime was for piano, jazz was for piano, Broadway was for piano, but nobody could wring a drop of juice out of rock on the piano. It was becoming a social dinosaur, soaking up living room space and useful only for supporting wedding and graduation photographs in filigreed silver frames. One by one the pianos began their outward journey, leaving no forwarding address.

As the '80s marched in, Junior quit practicing and his sister lay down her guitar: sound reproduction had taken a technological leap forward and left homegrown music dead in its wake. Why bother to learn to play when others already play so much better; when all we need is the right kind of speakers, and all it takes is money? And who would offend their ears with unprofessional sounds, when there's better stuff ready to hand? And as for "singing along," even those who used to ring a dozen changes on a dozen choruses of "Swing Low" are embarrassed to remember it. Can we ever have been so naive as to try to do it ourselves? Only at Christmastime, a small hard core sneaks out to the annual public sing-along of Handel's *Messiah,* where they slake their guilty thirst for singing with their fellow man, like wolves in a circle drawing satisfaction from their communal howls.

Living rooms were redecorated around the home

entertainment center, which once meant the piano, but the piano was gone, taking with it the pictures in filigreed frames and all those hundreds of songs that everyone knew. The corner tavern replaced its piano with a giant television screen for viewing football players larger than life and the drunks forgot the words to "The Whiffenpoof Song."

Probably it's all for the best, even if people rarely drop by to gather around our CD player now. The compact disc offers the finest professional performances in the world, reproduced so perfectly that listening is actually better than being there. Presumably we hear a lot more music now; heaven knows we spend enough money on it. We just don't feel like making our own anymore, after all those millennia, back to the days when we banged out the tempo with sticks on a rock, back to when field hands and miners sang their way home from work and everyone sang in the shower. Now we have waterproof radios and tape players to take over the chore while we soap up our flesh.

Professionals do it better. Why did we ever put up with those amateur aunts and uncles and neighbors around the baby grand, with a nephew to turn the pages, all belting out "God Rest Ye Merry, Gentlemen" on Christmas Eve? How could we have been so simpleminded such a short time ago?

PSYCHIATRISTS

FOR DECADES, YOU COULDN'T HOLD UP YOUR HEAD without one. "My analyst says . . . ," you offered airily, and strangers knew you immediately for a person of education and discernment. In urban areas, a psychiatrist was as essential as a dentist and a lot more fun to discuss.

A well-heeled young woman I knew upstaged us all by having two, one in New York and one in Philadelphia, and shuttled between them all week. At the office it was hard to arrange a meeting, since all the key people had standing dates with their analysts: A at two on Tuesdays and Thursdays, B at ten Monday, Wednesday, and Friday, C at four Tuesday and Friday. Good parents sent their children to special children's psychiatrists at the drop of a tantrum. In the *New York Times,* psychiatry bestrode both sides of the best-seller lists—novels, collections of case studies, sober expositions on the perilous road to mental health. Psychiatrists who held forth persuasively in print became celebrities and household words and their conclusions infallible, like the pope's. "Are you seeing a psychiatrist?" as a conversation opener would nowadays earn you a punch in the nose, but for fifty years it was a compliment. It meant, "One can plainly see you are sensitive, intense, and interesting, and therefore neurotic." Only the dullest of clods trudged around without a neurosis.

For those too young to remember, a bit of background. A neurosis was a social or sexual maladjustment, real or fancied. It could be anything from a fear of spiders to a lust for one of your parents. You took your neurosis to a psychiatrist to be cured. Psychiatry was invented by a man named Freud and was based on his theory that people had no way of knowing why they were unhappy or behaved peculiarly, because the origins of the problem were hidden from them, lurking in what he called the subconscious, and only a trained, expensive specialist could uncover and uproot them over the course of a long, expensive treatment. To try to get a grip on yourself yourself was hopeless, because nothing you thought you felt was what, deep down, you actually felt; in fact, usually quite the opposite. Nothing you remembered mattered, because the secret lay in what you'd deliberately forgotten ("repressed," it was called), and only a psychiatrist held the key.

Getting him to hand it over would cost you dearly. A few malcontents complained about the fortunes paid to an ordinary mortal to sit in a chair and listen to you for fifty minutes, but the psychiatrists explained that (a) they were not ordinary mortals, and (b) the expense was part of the therapy. If it came cheaper, it wouldn't do us any good.

Therapy came in two flavors. If you were a lowly peasant, you went with a specific problem and spent a few ad hoc sessions addressing it, much as we do today under managed health care, and hoped to be relieved of your most pressing symptoms, but you left knowing that vast interior wastelands remained unexplored, threatening to rise against you. If you claimed any sort of respectability at all, you went for the full psychoanalysis. This took years, but it left your system completely reamed and scoured, all its festering corners exposed to the healing sunshine of self-knowledge.

Your analyst would let you know when quitting time came, explaining that you were happy now, or as happy as you were going to get. The moment might coincide with his breaking point of boredom, when he couldn't listen to one more word out of you without screaming, or it might be the point when you and your relatives ran completely out of money. If you had plenty of money, the moment might never come.

No conceivable vice or habit has ever been as expensive as a good, thorough psychoanalysis. Several friends of mine had to leave their comfortable apartments and move into dank basement rooms, give up taxis, carry a sandwich for lunch, and switch from martinis to tap water. They loved every minute of it.

What was not to love? For several hours a week, a magically powerful person concentrated utterly upon you. To him or her you bared the wriggling, slimy, shameful creatures inhabiting your inmost swamps, and lo! he was not disgusted. Like God, he knew you better than you knew yourself, but unlike God he wasn't going to punish you. Under the rules of the game, nothing was your fault; all your sins had a cause—usually your mother—against which you'd been helpless.

Not only were you cleansed and made innocent, you were made important. However you might bore your friends and family, to be in analysis meant that, like the first rock brought back from Mars, you were worth analyzing. Unique, complex, fascinating. No longer a mere bookkeeper or housewife, you were an *analysand*.

Classically, you lay on a couch, with the analyst seated just out of sight beyond your head. This was supposed to conceal his reactions, perhaps his startled grimace when you confessed to some loathsome thought, but it may also have concealed him finishing

Sunday's Double Crostic. He may have been stifling yawns. He may have actually dozed off. You never knew. You never knew anything about him.

Psychiatrists lived fittingly separate from the world of patients; it would hardly do to have their worshipful clientele watching them try to start the lawn mower or hearing them scream at the kids. They all lived in the same suburb. They all belonged to the same country club. They vacationed at the same resorts, no doubt to insure the presence of intelligent life with which to hobnob, and they all arrived at them simultaneously on the first of August. Like Frenchmen, psychiatrists took the month of August off. In the cities they left behind, their patients fell slowly, dramatically to pieces without them. They twitched, woke howling from nightmares, bit their fingernails, chain-smoked, and yelled at their spouses. "My analyst's on vacation," they apologized. We understood.

What shrinks did on vacation was none of our business, and just as well. My friend Maggie was in analysis. Her husband, who thought psychiatry was hooey, complained bitterly about the bills, but Maggie maintained that her analyst was a sage of infinite wisdom and doing her a world of good. One August they stumbled by accident on her sage's vacation spot. Maggie should have kept her mouth shut, but she let out a small inadvertent shriek and cried, "There's Doctor_____!"

The good doctor was accompanied by a friend. They wore matching lavender bathing trunks, they were holding hands, and they were skipping—*skipping*—through the frothy waves. Maggie's husband was an old-fashioned and a conservative man, and he spoke politically incorrect words in ringing tones. Her analysis was abruptly

65

terminated, probably wrecking her chance of future sanity, but the bond had already been damaged.

The bond between patient and analyst (though not necessarily the reverse) was called transference, and it was passionate, intense, and sacred. You were not to dilute it by discussing your treatment with your other loved ones, even if they were paying his bills. As one in a trance, you were to follow while he led you into dark passages, holding aloft the torch of science.

Max, once a dear friend of mine, was the heart and glue of our circle of friends. He was warm, funny, affectionate, and sociable, and he held us together. He checked on us all regularly by phone, and on Sundays we all gathered at his apartment to help each other with the crossword puzzle and drink Bloody Marys. When ill or in trouble, we called Max first. When planning a party, we called Max first, and if he was otherwise engaged we changed the date.

Then he joined the throng on the couch. He went because, like all men at the time, he suspected himself of homosexual leanings and, like all men at the time, he knew psychiatry was the cure. Under the rule that whatever you thought you felt was the opposite of what you really felt, the more women you fell in love with, the more likely you were to be a repressed homosexual; overcompensating was the word.

Sexuality quite aside, his analyst led him to see that his whole life was a sham. Far from being kind and merry, friendly and sociable, he was actually overcompensating for a morose and sullen nature. He didn't, he learned, really like his friends at all; his affection was a mask for his hostility. With the expensive truth bared, rebellion was impossible. Obediently, Max changed. He stopped smiling. His face fell into different shapes, heavy and somber. Once he had known a hundred songs and belted them out joyfully on all occasions; he stopped singing. He stopped calling his friends. Nobody ever heard him laugh again. After a while it became quite thinkable, even desirable, to give a party without him.

You might question your dermatologist's diagnosis and get a second opinion, but you didn't question your shrink.

Then, deep into the rebellious '60s, the psychiatric moon began to wane. Its goal had always been the adjustment of the cranky and crooked to the socially normal, the shaping of the square peg to the round hole, and now people talked about changing the shape of the hole instead: society, far from being worthy of our adjustment, was a mess.

Women rebelled. It was Freud's contention that a woman who wanted to play the violin didn't really want a violin, she wanted a penis, and ought to get over it and go back to the kitchen. Women dropped their analysts and formed support groups, which were cheaper, and complained about men and took violin lessons. It was no longer chic to have a psychiatrist. It was chic to march on Washington, join civil rights groups, grow a beard, smoke pot, leap into bed with strangers, and bare as much of your psyche to casual acquaintances as you once had to your analyst.

Pills appeared. The lowliest family doctor could prescribe them, and it turned out that pills could soothe our anxieties, brighten our depressions, and level our mood swings without knowing the first thing about our relations with Mother. Stronger pills could even convince people that they weren't Napoleon Bonaparte or pursued by bat-shaped aliens.

The pills probably work better. Certainly they work faster. God knows they're cheaper. However, they struck a mighty blow to the self-esteem. On the couch, we were lords of a limitless underground kingdom of squalor and surprises that was ours alone. Now we're demoted to a skinful of predictable chemicals common to all; millions of us take the same Prozac, the same Valium, at the same moment every morning, to the same effect. The lurking tigers vanish from our closets, but their routing lacks the thrill of the chase. It's lonely, too. A pill pays no attention to our hidden motives and takes no notes on our troubles; we've all forgotten to remember our dreams, which were sometimes boring or frightening and sometimes enchanting fantasies we hadn't known we'd harbored, but there's no use telling them to a pill. It doesn't even know our name. The very word "dream" has retreated into advertising, as in, "Finally! The bathroom-bowl cleanser you've always dreamed of!"

And the psychiatrists themselves, once a whole social subset? A handful of them eke out a living as expert witnesses, testifying for the defense that the accused is barking mad or for the prosecution that he's no such thing, while the jury gets on with its knitting. Perhaps the younger ones retrained as computer technicians, since even the best-adjusted computer is a bundle of nerves and irrational impulses. The older ones have moved on by now, reminiscing about the glory days on that great golf course in the sky.

We miss them. They made us interesting to ourselves. Even in sleep we were interesting, seething with our unfathomable inner life. Now, though we may earn more money than Mike Tyson and own more gadgets than Bill Gates, deep down we know we're nothing special any more. Rather a bore, in fact. It's depressing.

LIQUOR CABINETS

"HOSPITABLE" WAS ONCE A HIGH-RANKING compliment, one of the nicest things you could say of people, redolent of all sorts of related traits like generosity, kindness, openness, and warmth. Hospitality, or flinging wide the door to friends and wayfarers alike, was once important, back in a world without motels or safety nets, where a friend might find his castle burnt down or a wayfarer find bandits on his trail. This free offering of food and drink and shelter was built into the social contract and the Old Testament, and besides, the host might be in mortal need of it himself someday: life was chancy.

Life got safer, but the habit of easy hospitality persisted until late in the twentieth century. The phrase "Why don't you stop by for a drink?" fell lightly from the lips in those days, before a drink became a sign of mental illness. Food might or might not be included; a bowl of potato chips or a dish of peanuts could stand in as symbolic of food, actual food being labor-intensive, but the heart of hospitality was the liquor cabinet.

In modest households it might simply be one of the kitchen cupboards set aside for the purpose. In others it was freestanding, and in one grand menage I frequented, a broad low door in the living room wall concealed a trolley fitted for bottles, ice bucket, cocktail shaker, and glassware in the correct shapes for every known libation; it was wheeled forth among the guests like a roasted ox and the host manned it as if conducting an orchestra. (When the owners, now old, die and new

69

people move in, I suppose they will throw away the trolley and use its space for boots and umbrellas.) During Prohibition, liquor cabinets were disguised as nonalcoholic furniture, or hidden behind faux bookcases, like a safe; one family I know had a splendid pool table installed and concealed the bar in a panel behind the rack of cues.

For those of modest means, the minimum stores required by the most basic hospitality were Scotch, bourbon, vodka, gin, vermouth, and one or more of the heavily advertised blended whiskeys, with additions depending on one's acquaintanceship; if a guest had asked in vain for rum, the next time he stopped by there would be rum. Supplies stored elsewhere included cold beer, generous amounts of ice, quinine water (to be mixed with gin or vodka), soda water (to be mixed with Scotch), lemons and limes, and olives, which were added to martinis, which were a varying combination of gin or vodka and vermouth. None of this was purchased for the occasion, since the occasions were spontaneous and often unexpected. It was kept on hand.

For those under forty, this must seem a staggering nuisance and expense, quite aside from the immorality of it, but for those bred in the tradition it was simply an essential domestic supply, like coffee and bread, but promising far more entertainment.

In far-off times, the company of other people provided most of the entertainment most people got. For the isolated country household, a rain-soaked traveler stopping by for a slug of mead or brandy and a drying by the hearth brought news of kings and battles and the reassurance that the world was still in motion. For the young and single, ten to eighty years ago, a chattering crowd of friends stopping by for a pitcher of martinis

70

brought light and color and fresh jokes to the dreary studio apartment. The liquor cabinet was the hearth at which they warmed themselves. Its contents, prudently consumed, melted social barriers, inspired the shy, and fueled spirited discussions of the meaning of life.

"Some people are coming over for drinks," the host or hostess would say, "and there's someone I think you should meet." Nowadays this would mean a possible business contact, but in the bad old days it meant possible romance. This custom gave the prospective pair a couple of hours to check each other out, risk free, in the easy company of mutual friends. If it clicked, fine; if not, no hard feelings. It was infinitely pleasanter than the stiff, lonely, precarious "dating" of recent times. It was even fun. Ask among the older generations and you'll find an astonishing number of happy couples who met each other at the liquor cabinets of friends. The fall of the liquor cabinet coincided with the rise of the "personal" ads. This is not progress.

For the married couple, dropping in or being dropped in on for a drink provided a revitalizing change of voices and faces and viewpoints, not to mention people about whom to speculate later. After the guests departed, the man of the house checked the levels in the various bottles to see which needed replenishment; it was one of his domestic duties, often the only one besides making martinis.

Connoisseurs of stylish living from Nick Charles to James Bond recognized the martini, whether shaken or stirred, as a gender-specific art form, and for decades every man who aspired to sophistication worked to perfect his product. Unlike the perfect soufflé, it was created under the gaze of the guests (only a slob would make and refrigerate a pitcherful in advance; the alchemy would dissipate) and was largely performance art, a form of swordplay for the urban male. While measuring and shaking or stirring, he was expected to say a few words to the audience about his proportions and whether or not he believed that gin was bruisable. However witty and attractive his wife might be, this was the moment of the man, and all eyes were upon him. If the guests had all opted for Scotch instead, the host, not to be robbed of his limelight moment, made a martini for himself, reconsecrating the altar of the liquor cabinet.

My aunt and uncle had a particularly pretty and generous liquor cabinet, in polished birch with carved curving legs. It lived in the dining room. One dark afternoon I went to pay them a Christmas call, bringing along a new boyfriend to introduce. They offered us a drink, of course; back then it was unthinkable not to, at any hour after three or so, and "She didn't even offer me a drink" described the sharpest slap of rejection.

The four of us sat around the table drinking, and somehow the talk turned to absinthe. Uncle Bob said he thought he had some, a bottle brought by a friend from Switzerland long ago, when you could still buy it there if you had the right contacts. He rummaged in the cabinet, back beyond the basics, and came out with a bottle of ancient French brandy, dusty and almost empty, and Bols gin in a stoneware crock. He set out some more glasses and we tried them while he dug deeper. He hauled forth souvenirs of old friends and old voyages; tawny port, and potent smoky Scotch from some hidden glen, Spanish sherry, applejack with a hand-printed label, unsanitized tequila with a look of murder in its eye, slivovitz with a label in Polish, aquavit smelling like rye bread, hundred-proof Cuban rum dark as sin, and liqueurs brewed by monks according to secret recipes half as old as time and tasting of mint, or flowers, or bitter oranges. The table grew a forest of bottles. By all rights the combinations should have made us sick as cats, but somehow the cheer of the moment preserved us in health and merriment.

There was no absinthe. Some unsupervised guest at some merry party must have been tempted by its reputation and rarity, Toulouse-Lautrec's viciously seductive Green Fairy, for whose favors men had beggared themselves and gone mad. In the farthest corner, however, was an unlabeled Mason jar that Bob brought out, like a conjurer of many rabbits, marveling. "I remember this," he said. "Moonshine. We bought it from the fellow who made it, on our honeymoon, back before the War, in the Smoky Mountains. He swore it was the best in Tennessee."

We passed it around, sniffing it respectfully, but none of us had the courage to try it. Inspired, Aunt Peggy poured out a saucerful and touched it with a match. It burned clean and hot, with a bright blue dancing flame, until it had burned away. Awed, we each touched the saucer with a fingertip and yes, it was dry. "Pure and unadulterated," said Bob proudly. "The best in Tennessee."

They flicked their eyes briefly at each other, remembering their wedding trip, and my boyfriend gazed at me with new respect, coming as I did from a family with Aladdin's own cave of hospitality in their dining room.

"Hospitable" is now a word used mainly by hotels and resorts, and a hostess is the lady who walks you to your table. As modern Americans we probably prefer it that way, being more comfortable with what we've paid for in a straight business transaction than with what's been offered freely but may carry some nebulous obligation in its wake. Here and there, though, the tradition survives, at least by hearsay.

The young are understandably confused by the difference between friends dropping by and the full-blown cocktail party. The latter required advance invitation and was an efficient way to pay off social obligations to people to whom you owed less than an actual dinner. Since many of the guests would be strangers to each other, the rule was to have more people than places to sit, if necessary hiding the chairs in the bedroom, so folks would mill around, clutching drinks and cheese crackers, and "mix."

They were invited for five till seven and expected to show up around six and clear out by eight-thirty.

Recently, in one of the country's most sophisticated newspapers, I read a column explaining what a cocktail party was and how, in the long-ago times, people gathered together to use alcohol. In case the reader might like to re-create such a funny old custom, the writer included recipes for several complicated canapés and, for the proffered cocktail, a pitcher of "sangria" consisting almost entirely of fruit, soda water, and ice cubes. No liquor cabinet was mentioned. No liquor was mentioned. We live now in enlightened times.

The footsore pilgrim of old, the wayfarer half frozen from the storm, the tongue-tied lover dropping nervously by, might or might not be glad to hear it.

PORCHES

MY GRANDMOTHER'S HOUSE, IN A SLEEPY SUBURB of Washington, had three porches: the essential front porch, without which a house could hardly call itself a house, and in back, a screened porch for summer meals and, over it, a screened sleeping porch, where children were laid on warm nights to listen to windfall apples thunking down into the grass.

A screened porch was private and considered part of the house. Although we were perfectly visible eating or reading there, no neighbor would come over and start a conversation through the screening, which functioned as a transparent wall with breezes blowing through it. Front porches were never screened. People on front porches were in a semipublic state, midway between house and street, and open for a bit of a chat.

There was more foot traffic in those days, and sidewalks were laid down to accommodate it. Nowadays, where sidewalks survive they seem an anachronism, quaint as an oil lamp, but up until recently people used them to come and go on errands or to stroll around the block in the cool of the evening, after dinner, greeting neighbors on porches. In 1900, President McKinley's entire campaign for re-election consisted of sitting on his front porch greeting the passersby.

Unless the passerby was invited to come and join the sitters, conversations were expected to be brief, on the order of, "Is Johnny feeling better?" or "Think we'll ever get some rain?" There was no obligation to issue an invitation; the fleeting nature of the encounter was taken for granted. If the invitation was, however, extended and accepted, there was plenty of room. Porches were big, built to include neighbors, and usually held either a two-seater swing suspended from the ceiling or a glider, a sort of weatherproof couch that moved gently back and forth, with assorted extra seating in wicker. Iced tea or coffee might be served, if handy, but unlike the guest within the actual house, the porch guest expected no solid refreshment.

For the porch's owners, it served as a kind of safety valve for the house. It was both home and not-home. A child feeling oppressed could go sulk on the porch without the inconvenience of actually running away. A housewife, lonely and isolated, could go sit on the glider, outside in the world, and snap beans or sew with an eye out for a passing neighbor and a greeting or two. On rainy days, when the house walls closed in on its inhabitants, they could sit on the porch and see the world without getting wet. On hot days, they could sit in the shade of the porch and catch any breeze that came by, lighting a citronella candle to fend off mosquitoes as evening fell, waiting for the house to cool off. For a girl coming home from an evening out, the porch was where she was kissed good night, and its swing or glider was where she was kissed further, until her parents, sensing mischief, flicked the light off and on to drive the twain asunder.

Porches were, and still are where they still exist and haven't been glassed in as sunrooms, seasonally decorated. Pots of red geraniums in the summer, yellow chrysanthemums in fall; flags for Memorial Day; swags of bunting for the Fourth of July; sheaves of corn and rows of jack-o'-lanterns for Halloween. At Christmas, colored lights strung along their edges, a wreath on the door, and holly wrapped around the railing with red ribbons. The decorations were a greeting from the private family within to the public family beyond, signifying goodwill to neighbor and passerby and membership in the larger world beyond the parlor.

New suburban houses have decks. A deck is a completely different concept, a platform behind the house, screened from the neighbors by bush, tree, and trellis and reached not by way of the public street but by passing through the private area; only the formally invited can tread thereon or even suspect its existence. Instead of greeting the world, it hides and throws up defenses.

A deck is roofless, exposed to the midday sun and the sudden thunderstorm that drowns the barbecue coals. Few people sit on their decks. Compared to porches, they're lonely places. Besides, air-conditioning has depopulated summer and altered the American metabolism until we take no pleasure in heat; our flesh treats it as an assault, like winter's blasts. Most decks are used exclusively by the barbecue grill, which provides the only contact with the neighbors as the scent of charcoal-lighter fluid unites us under its pall and the smoke of our chicken drifts next door to blend companionably with the smoke of the neighbors' steak.

We have sealed ourselves up in airtight containers. Even our cars are hidden from the world in locked garages, and driving through the gracefully curving streets of a new subdivision on a sunny Saturday, past the blankfaced houses, we have no way of knowing whether anyone lives there at all. Indoors, the private family has no way of knowing whether there's anyone out beyond their walls or whether, just possibly, they're all alone in the world.

CITIES

OUR CITIES STILL SIT WHERE THEY ALWAYS SAT, BUT now they're usually referred to as "inner cities," to distinguish their schools, crime, and income levels from those of the encircling rings of suburbs reaching away to the horizon. Embedded in the suburbs are the "edge cities," former suburbs or small towns now blossoming into vertical concrete slabs of offices and horizontal concrete acres of shopping malls.

Over half of us now live in a suburb. We fling ourselves farther and farther from the center, out across the former cornfields, with the energy once devoted to moving the other direction, into the center of everything that mattered. Our forebears decanted themselves from caravans, wagons, coaches, ships, and trains, and saw the cathedral on the hill over the marketplace and heard its carillon singing and rejoiced: they were here! Now we keep beating our way back, ten miles at a time, along the road we came.

Once people out beyond the cities longed for them. Half sick with boredom, farm and village adolescents tossed in their beds and yearned to be in Babylon, Troy, Athens, Rome, Constantinople, Paris, Delhi, Damascus, London, Chicago, San Francisco, far from familiar faces, cows and crops and weather and gossiping neighbors. They longed for crowds of strangers, for noise and lights and happenings, as the drowning long for air. Sentimentalists like Wordsworth lamented that wholesome country boys went to the city and fell headfirst into the fleshpots, forgot their pious raising, and lost their souls in tavern and theater, maybe lost even their virginities, so troublesome to lose at home, but for some reason the lads were undismayed and continued to set out, like Dick Whittington, earthly possessions wrapped in a shawl, to seek their fortunes and whatever else was on the menu. Corruption was half the fun. Early in the first century A.D., there were thirty-two thousand prostitutes on the police register in Rome. In the 1890s there were officially thirty-five thousand in New York. Nobody counted the amateurs.

The cities were dirty and dangerous; how would they not be? Except for a few obsessives like the Romans, sanitation wasn't high on the list of concerns, and any pickpocket with sense would prefer city work to the countryside, where nobody carried cash and everybody went to bed at dark. Cities were unhealthy; plagues swept through the crowds and carried off half the population. New people rushed to take their places. Where else was there to be?

The cathedral was in the city, and the parish priest longed for the power in its corridors. The king lived in the city, surrounded by courtiers; the petty nobility, rusticating obscurely on their country estates, longed to rub elbows at court with the influential, while the lads and lasses longed to work for royalty in stable or kitchen and watch and gossip. Lawyers clustered around the courts, scholars around the universities. Apprentices came to learn a trade. Merchants built grand houses, and money scented the air like spices. Ships sailed into the port bearing wonders from far away, and the marketplace was a jabbering international festival of vendors, jewelers, weavers, goldsmiths, vegetables, donkeys, coffeehouses, rugs, swords, fishwives, and open sewers. Caravans of dark strangers in strange clothes came from across the desert. There were processions and riots, coronations and hangings, actors, thieves, lights, music, and a market for everyone's wares and skills. Something different happened every day. For the young from the monotonous country world, that alone was worth the price of one's virtue.

Ever since the Mesopotamian centers of Sumer and Ur, each country's culture lived in its principal city, because for a culture to have any impact it needs a concentrated mass; lone voices scattered in the provinces wield no clout. Luckily for us, young Will Shakespeare looked around at the charming village of Stratford-upon-Avon, wrapped up a change of underwear, and legged it for London, as those before and after him rushed to their cities and huddled in alehouses or on street corners and argued philosophy, sneered at each other's paintings, fomented revolutions, and hobnobbed generally, drawing strength from each other's company.

Cities inspired loyalty, and each man felt his own the best, as a citizen of Rome walked the empire caparisoned in pride and privilege. It was easier to feel patriotism for a city than for a whole sprawling country, much of which you'd never seen; a city was a manageable concept to be grasped and owned with pride. Up until recently, every city had its unique signature, a style of architecture, a peculiar food sold on street corners, a fabulously unlucky baseball team, a product, an attitude. As Venice had its canals, Chicago had gangland shootings, New Orleans had decadence and balconies, Boston had Puritans banning books. Families stayed in the same city, often the same section of the same city, for generations, loyal as dogs, unable to conceive of life elsewhere, and on their way to work passed their old elementary school and the church where their grandparents were married.

I grew up in a suburb, where the streets were safe and the people similar and nothing ever happened at all, and the city at the far end of the avenue always whistled in my ear. Washington was small then, considered boring by the cosmopolitan and with few proud idiosyncrasies to flourish, but things happened there. When I was thirteen and fourteen, my friend and I would take the bus down the avenue, sometimes ignoring school for the afternoon, and get off and wander the streets; children in those days weren't so closely supervised and could go where they pleased as long as they were home in time for dinner. Gloria and I prowled the city on foot, watching, listening. sniffing, and tasting. We knew the free Smithsonian museums like our living rooms, and we knew where to find used bookstores, cheap street food, and quarters where the passersby were Chinese or Greek or Arabic; we sniffed in the doorways of their restaurants and touched the foreign vegetables and artifacts for sale on their sidewalks and listened to their mysterious words. In the suburbs, everywhere you go you're trespassing, but a city is public property; if you're there, it's yours, and we set our feet down on our city as firmly as kings. It wasn't a great city, but it beat the peace and quiet of Chevy Chase: it was Life. Someday, we told each other, we would live in a great one. Bombay, maybe. Alexandria. Venice. Someplace slightly sinister, with trouble always brewing. Rio. Barcelona. Istanbul. We recited their names, trying to decide; at fourteen all things are possible.

In our more sensible moments, we realized that if we wanted to make names for ourselves (and we did), it would have to be New York. New York, at midcentury, was the only place to go for names. Chicago was proud to call itself the Second City; nobody asked who was first.

For a hundred and fifty years New York was the navel of the world. At its pinnacle it combined the principal glories of Babylon, Rome, and Athens at their own pinnacles. Like Babylon, it was Sin City, flaunting exotic options in wickedness that, merely to consider them down on the farm, addled the wits of preacher and farm boy alike. Like Rome, it was the seat and center of power and its empire girdled the earth; the New York Stock Exchange ruled; everyone of any importance sooner or later had to come to New York, as they'd gone to Rome, to seal his importance; no hero was truly a hero until the tickertape parade. And like Athens, it was culture's home and marketplace, shedding its pure astringent light on the world's art.

If you had a talent to sell, New York was where you took it. Nothing else counted. A gallery show, a concert, or a play successful "out of town," with raves in the out-of-town papers, simply didn't count; only New York and the godlike New York critics could pass judgment. Musicians dreamed of Carnegie Hall, by way of the glittering nightclubs. Poets and painters dreamed of life in the Village. Actors and dancers and playwrights dreamed of Broadway, and even if they'd made a name in the movies, the name remained slightly bogus until authenticated in New York. Even the Hollywood filmmakers themselves dreamed of the film festival at Lincoln Center, perhaps feeling a little marginal, so far away out west. Novels set anywhere beyond the five boroughs were dismissed as "regional novels." In proper novels, set in New York, minor characters might be identified only by their addresses, and if a reader didn't know what it meant to live in Queens or on Riverside Drive or Sutton Place, then that reader was of no consequence.

New York was national headquarters and very little outside it was of any consequence. No New Yorker ever said he was going to be in Paris or Hong Kong next week; he said he was going to be out of town. Even failures who never touched even the tail feathers of their dreams, however feeble, despised, and lowly they might be, could hold their heads up over the rest of the world: they were New Yorkers.

There was an elusive quality then, long since out of style, called sophistication. The word is now used primarily to describe computer software, but for a time it was personal. It stood for a complex of how to live and look, what to eat and drink and think and say, what to read and write. Who to be. It meant the wicked quips at the Algonquin's round table; cartoons in the old *New Yorker* magazine. It was the opposite of sentimental, so that its enemies called it heartless and shallow, but these were the jealous outsiders who could never attain it. Sophistication called for a variety of talents and attitudes, but the minimum requirement was being in New York. Not all New Yorkers achieved it, but nobody elsewhere had a prayer. The would-be sophisticate of Chicago or San Francisco was but a country cousin of the real thing. As with money and fame, if you wanted it, New York was where you went to get it.

Up until 1980 or so, the brawls and hijinks and watering holes of Manhattan's artists and writers and painters made national news. It may be that they're still brawling and watering and we don't care anymore, or they may have straggled off separately to the suburbs, or withered away from sheer apathy. Or gone to Hollywood, apparently our last outpost of the creative life. As the century waned, even the most ardent New

Yorkers looked around and saw a kind of shabbiness at the heart of their town. The soul was fading. Babylonian sin became politically incorrect and Athenian culture elitist and beside the point, and even the Roman power was fragmenting; people started speaking seriously of faraway places like Houston and even places that could hardly be called places at all, like Redmond, Washington.

Perhaps New York wasn't, after all, the navel of the world and the gorgeous coat of many colors in which they wished to dress their children. Maybe it was only an office. Families who had lived in town for a hundred years journeyed beyond its borders to look at real estate. Every year a hundred thousand New Yorkers move out.

Everywhere now, long before sunrise, the headlights of sleepy commuters swarm toward their offices, and long after dark swarm back to the suburbs again.

Committees are appointed to dress up the remains of the cities as theme parks for tourists. New York's mayor trumpets proudly that the murder rate, always a drawback for theme parks, has fallen dramatically, but the old New Yorkers had taken a kind of pride in it, feeling it proved their courage and loyalty and the wimpiness of those who lived elsewhere. Pornography has been driven out of town and the once world-class possibilities for sin have dwindled to smoking a cigarette in public. Times Square and Forty-second Street, long metaphors for exciting sleaze, have been laundered into an outpost of the Disney empire. Officials hail this as a great step forward, but to a morose few it feels like a long slide down from the kingdom of grown-ups to the Magic Kingdom. New York was where we wanted to live when we were finally grown up, and drink martinis and stay out past bedtime, not where we wanted to take the toddlers for a weekend of family values.

In cities all over the world, dramatic old buildings fall into disrepair, to be replaced by office towers like concrete tombstones or expensively restored, with a gift shop, to lure the tourist. Great chunks of inner cities are bulldozed to make room for convention centers, stadiums, and entertainment complexes for visitors, but visitors, however many hot dogs they may buy, do not a city make. Nobody wanted to live next to a slum, but nobody wants to live in a sports stadium either.

Those who come to a city come by car and leave again by car, and what they see, in New York or London or Rome or Paris, is mostly other cars. The former residents flee in cars.

And out beyond the shrinking cities, in the burgeoning suburbs, monotonous miles of ugliness pound us over the head on our daily rounds and we take no notice. We've developed a resistance to it, and ugliness no longer has any meaning and certainly wouldn't affect our choice of what to build, any more than boredom affects our choice of where to live. Without our electronic home entertainment, we'd choke to death on boredom out there, like the farmers' sons of yore, but still we keep streaming away from the center.

Our forebears, yearning their eyes over the last hill for the first glimpse of cathedral and university and marketplace, would think we'd gone mad.

WINDOWS

I'M NOT QUALIFIED TO DISCUSS EMISSIONS, OZONE, pollen, airborne particulates, or industrial pollutants, but I'm beginning to think they don't matter anymore: who breathes raw air?

Hotels, offices, and public buildings have been sealed up for decades now, lest some rash fool be tempted to subvert the ordained temperature or sneak an illicit cigarette. The air that was impounded within their walls when the walls went up thirty years ago is still miraculously transparent, after having been inhaled and exhaled many millions of times. Last year's flu germs have probably died of old age, and the ducts stand ready for this year's; the ducts have seen flus come and seen them go. The windows have gazed impassively out on blizzard and heat wave and balmy May morning, unmoved.

At even the quaintest of bed-and-breakfasts, out in the grassy countryside, the windows are imbedded in the walls; the traveler can only press his nose to the glass and peer through it at the mountain views and wonder how the flowers smell and whether there's an owl hooting somewhere. The air is provided by the establishment, included in the price of the room. Somewhere, known only to the proprietor, out of sight and out of reach, is a control switch, and the weather report or the calendar will tell her when to flip it from "cool" to "heat."

Most people are used to it now, and even like it; they always know what to expect from the air. Like a packaged soup mix, it's been quality-controlled, and it's not going to change at some climatic whim, or blow the papers off the desk. Standardized air smooths out their mood swings; no more the daydreaming languors of June, the restless busyness of October, the foreboding before a storm, harking for distant thunder; no more the quick dash to close up against the coming rain. All days are reassuringly alike.

A few misfits feel a creeping unease, the itch of claustrophobia, and can't sleep. The sealed house seems to be covering its ears and holding its breath. The more neurotic among us think of being buried alive; we can almost hear the thud of clods on the coffin over our heads.

I know a capable young woman who carries with her everywhere a package of what she calls burglar's tools, in case she needs to fix her transmission en route or finds a piano in want of tuning. She and her young man had found a small hotel for the weekend, far from the madding crowd, and checked in hoping to spend the night lulled by the wind in the pine trees. Their bedroom was all that could be desired, with a basin on the washstand and a quilt on the four-poster bed, but the windows were sealed shut. Under them, metal devices poured forth a gale of bitterly conditioned air, smelling of antique dust.

Her young man was furious, and threatened to check out again and look further, but Alix whipped out her tools. In minutes she'd removed the windows from their frames and propped them against the wall. Then she managed to disable the conditioning units without having to break them. Then they slept like kittens, the breezes washing around their bed and smelling of pine trees. In the morning, refreshed, she helped a stray butterfly outside and put the windows back in their frames and turned the conditioning back on to chill the next traveler's bones.

Car windows are still movable, so the driver can say, "Fill it up with regular" without having to shout, but most drivers switch the lever from heat to cool as the seasons change. Dirt blows in, they say, if you open the windows, and busy highways smell carcinogenic. Best to have reliable air, air you can count on, processed air.

I'm not against air-conditioning. I'm told it's done wonders for productivity in the American South, and I'm sure that's true. Just think of the sufferings of southerners, way back when. They had to get up early in the fresh mornings and do as much work as possible before the day steamed up. Then, like the natives in Noel Coward's "Mad Dogs and Englishmen," they would *put their Scotch or rye down/And lie down.* They retreated to the shade of maple tree or summerhouse, porch or balcony or shuttered parlor with ceiling fans revolving. They napped, or wrote up their diaries, or picked out a few tunes, blotted their brows from time to time, and gossiped with the neighbors over lemonade until cool evening fell and shutters were opened to the breeze. One's heart bleeds for them. Now, with conditioned air, they get to work in windowless offices all day long, all year round, like everyone else. No doubt they're grateful.

So rich are the blessings of air control that even many new private houses are eliminating the alternative. I was in one the other day. It was one of the imposing minimansions springing up all over the countryside where cows used to graze, here in a land that all early travelers praised for the sweetness of its climate and the healthful, restorative qualities of its air, and it was sealed shut. Designed for cuttingedge energy efficiency, it sported maximum insulation and the last word in air processors busily scrubbing and rinsing the stuff and sending it back ready to be breathed again, though the structure was so well sealed that too deep a breath might implode the walls. Windows—now called "fixed glass"—admitted light but no leak of alien air, and as my host proudly pointed out, no dust, so the house stayed cleaner. Through the glass I could see the narrow strip of woods the developer had left, with a stream twisting through it. Any possible rustle of water or whistle of bird was kept out there where it belonged.

Mind you, there was nothing wrong with the air in the house. It didn't smell of stale wood smoke or boiled cabbage, as houses did at the end of along winter in bygone days. It was just inert. Sanitary, I'm sure, but without meaning or messages. When I stepped outside again and breathed, it was like stroking a live cat after stroking a stuffed one.

I don't know what happened to the concept of oxygen. In my childhood, it was considered important to health and even to life; it was why miners carried canaries down into the airless depths. We were told that in a confined area, the oxygen could be "used up" by repeated breathing. We were sent outdoors to play in it. At night, our bedroom windows were opened, even if only a crack, so it could come in. Sleeping in a closed room, breathing the same air over and over, was considered quite disgustingly unwholesome, akin to drinking our bathwater. Air, it was understood, needed constant refreshment.

Windows were originally holes in the walls to let in light, so you could see to chop the turnips without wasting candles. When it got too cold you closed them, more or less, with shutters, and lit a candle. The busy Romans developed glass windows, which were an improvement except for the poor, who went on using oiled paper. Plenty of fresh air leaked in through the walls. Presently the casement window arrived, and then the sash window, and then screening to keep out wildlife. On the first warm day of spring, windows were flung open and the curtains billowed and everyone rejoiced in the fresh infusion of enzymes, or ions, or ideas, or whatever unfettered air contains, and word came in from the great world—traffic, children, roosters, sirens, planes, and the smell of cut grass. Women, housebound by their duties, leaned out of open windows into the world, gossiping with neighbors, checking on the children, calling out messages, or placing orders with a passing peddler.

Now we just dial the thermostat to "spring." Change over from "humidify" to "dehumidify." We're in charge in here. Only controlled sounds can be heard, issuing from our own compact discs, our own cat, our own properly identified friends and family. No random uninvited cry ruffles our sealed world, no smell we don't understand, no breeze we didn't order.

The only people exposed to uncontrolled air now are the remaining cigarette smokers, forced out to the parking lot or the back steps in the uncooled, unheated, arid or humid world, inhaling their carcinogens along with the vital and mysterious essence.

One of our planet's two great blessings is a breathable atmosphere, and we seem to be turning our backs on it. Are we unconsciously preparing ourselves for life on the moons of Jupiter, where no birds sing and an air leak in the walls would kill us? Or do we so dislike our neighbors now that we won't share our air with them? Or is it the whole great random uncontrollable world we're sealing out of our lives? Are we frightened of something out there? Or are we no longer curious about that which isn't us?

For that matter, why should windows even be transparent? Plenty of state-of-the-art lighting indoors, far more reliable than sunshine, and the view is probably depressing. The billowing gauzy curtain has yielded to the "window treatment," involving three or four layers of blinds, inner curtains, outer draperies, and valances, to ward off the world.

Why have windows at all, when they're useful only to burglars?

When the movable glass window arrived, it must have seemed as happy an invention as the roof. But then, the flyswatter was a fine invention too, and we don't need that anymore either.

FACTORIES

DURING WORLD WAR II, EVERY FLAT SURFACE bloomed with signs and ads and posters showing factories belching smoke. We shall make guns and tanks, cried the message. See our factories! We are strong! We shall win! After the war (which we did win), more ads and posters showed more factories belching a more peaceable smoke, often with a train curving around them, also belching smoke, which in those days meant power and progress rather than pollution: We shall prosper! We shall make all manner of things and live the good life! Great is America!

We were urged to "buy American," both patriotically, to boost prosperity, and sensibly, because American-made goods were better than anyone else's. My grandmother, shopping, always checked credentials and looked for the union label, the ILGWU tag that meant it wasn't made in a foreign sweatshop by six-year-old orphan slaves. Cars and refrigerators and shoes and pots and pans poured from assembly lines across America. It was called "Better things for better living," in a phrase that now sounds almost heartbreaking in its innocence. We made things. Things were good.

Then the smoke began to thin. War forgotten, we bought cars from Germany, then from Japan, and clothes from southeast Asian countries we'd never heard of before. The Rust Belt appeared, and spread. Industry, once a high and noble calling, began to seem dirty and sweaty and a bit old-fashioned; it was time for something new. We were told we had now evolved into the Post-Industrial Age, and would henceforth be a "service economy," a phrase that made some people think of a nation of parlor maids and messenger boys and didn't have quite the muscular impact of "industry."

Then we were told instead that we were entering the Space Age, about to shuffle off this earthly coil and leap weightlessly into the stars, and this sounded much more glamorous than service. On closer inspection, however, the Space Age was seen not to affect most of us personally: we could check it out on television, but as a lifestyle option it proved elusive.

What was next? Who were we about to be? Quite suddenly, as evolutions go, computers leaped onto center stage and within a few years became the driving force of our national life. We'd answered the question. Our postindustrial world would be the Information Age, our national product "information management." Anything else we needed would come from places where English is not spoken and the instructions for assembly and operation would be written in words that sounded hauntingly familiar but could not be construed.

Information doesn't have the solidity of industry or the romance of space, but at least it brought us a new toy. Schools replaced the moldy old books with computers; education now consists of learning to use them. In ads for home computers, we see Mom and Dad and Heather gathered 'round, all laughing like hyenas with joy, while Heather at the keyboard frolics in the fields of information. Information access will make Heather rich and successful, while our new immigrants, once the muscle behind prosperity, wander the streets bewildered and useless, unable to click a mouse, and are forced into driving taxis before they can understand English or know what city they've landed in.

America will lead the world in information, though as a source of national pride it's hard to get a grip on. It was a prideful thing to say we built the best cars in the world, as a country might say it wove the most beautiful rugs or produced the richest milk in the world, but how shall we measure which country manages the best information?

As always, I find myself wallowing in the backwaters behind the curve. Far behind the curve. It's too late now to go around buttonholing people and asking, "This information highway we're all hurtling down, does it *go* anywhere, or is the journey the whole point? And for that matter, *what the hell is information?*"

Even while I am pondering this, my neighbor comes to the door with a petition to sign. He wants me to protest against children in our public libraries accessing pornography at our expense, and I'm not quite sure how I feel about this, but I'm fond of my neighbor and I sign. Then I fall to wondering about the evils of censorship, weighed against the evils of porn on the Net, information red in tooth and claw. Just how corrupting is it, and as an exparent, how horrified would I have been to find my tots in the library learning peculiar and unsettling things about sex?

When my neighbor is safely down the lane, I check to make sure I'm alone, call up Infoseek, and ask it, "What is fellatio?"

I get 9,677,994 answers to check out.

Clearly my neighbor has a point; this must be more than any tot needs to know. Imagine not just one's personal youthful confusions about sex, but a choice of ten million confusions. I roll up my sleeves and plunge into the teeming cesspool, and the first source offered under "fellatio" is a surgically precise description of gay and lesbian sex practices and the props thereof, much more offputting than exciting, with warnings about which objects not to insert in the anus. The second click brings us a hiphop band called the Mountain Brothers in Philadelphia that claims connection with a spiritual group of brothers on a mountain in ancient China and offers enlightenment as well as song. The third selection is about conducting job interviews, exploring one's career goals, accessing career information, and networking for jobs. The fourth is packed with useful links in linguistics, prehistoric languages, dialects, and phonemes. The fifth is on how to buy a Fannie Mae-owned property and the legal precautions to observe when considering the purchase of a fore-closed home. With the sixth, we're back to sex, with words in five languages for the traveler: "hug," "friend," "date," "kiss," "bedroom," "mouth," and a word which in French is "heterosexual," but translates into English as "eterosexual." This is offered to facilitate international dating, but without verbs it's not going to get you very far.

Then we slip off the point again. The seventh juice nugget is a detailed record of everything Speaker of the House Newt Gingrich has been doing for the past few months, mercifully none of it relevant.

Whatever you're selling, file it under sex and the

customers will come. I realize there are well over nine million more sources to check and some of them may be more titillating, but life is short. I open my battered paperback dictionary. It feels reassuringly solid in my hand, softened with long use, and it tells me, in eight easily accessed words, what fellatio is.

All of which leaves the definition of information open. Is it interchangeable? Is information on whales the same as information on job interviews? Should I be satisfied with whatever I get? Is it useful just because it's information? "Knowledge" I understand. "Wisdom" is a word now used only by best-selling gurus peddling mystic platitudes; I think it used to mean knowledge raised to an almost spiritual level of certainty. But what are we supposed to do with this information stuff?

I go back to seek scholarly facts. At random, I ask Yahoo about Amelia Earhart. And there indeed she is, information at my fingertips. A brief biography, followed by eight related topics. The biography is tough reading. Paragraph two tells me, "Alfred was never impressed with who he considered the 'ne'er do well' son-in-law, Edwin." Paragraph four contains the sentence, "He and Amy moving to Des Moines, leaving the girls with their grandparents in Atchison." Who writes the road signs on this highway? Anybody? Or does the computer itself generate them somehow? Not that it matters; information, not grammar, is the point. I move on to the related topics, two of them about planes and three about one Linda Finch, who set out to complete Earhart's last journey. Did she make it? Alas, Ms. Finch is "not found on this server." I log off, feeling unfulfilled.

I've been seduced into buying the *Encyclopedia Britannica* on a shiny disk that fits into the computer. It took up far less room than the real thing, and I was assured it was infinitely superior, containing 66,000 entries and 44 million words, which you must admit is a whole bunch of information. It is, I was told, appropriate for "serious scholarship," another phrase that's come down in the world socially. I broke the computer trying to install the thing, but my trusty repairman came and fixed it.

One of its greatest glories, this disk, is that it offers you a generous helping of related topics to enrich your serious scholarship. I ask it, too, for Amelia Earhart. It produces a terse, four-paragraph biography and nine related topics: Llanelli is a county in Wales with rolling hills and a coastline, in which Earhart once landed by mistake; Howland Island is where she failed to land on the last trip, and small wonder, it's a mile and a half long and half a mile wide; Charles Lanier Lawrance was an aeronautical engineer; Amelia Jenks Bloomer, long before Earhart's day, invented bloomers; bloomers were the floppy pants Amelia Jenks invented; Ludwig yon Siegen was a seventeenth-century German painter; Henry Fielding was an eighteenth-century English novelist; Seneca Falls, New York, was the home of Amelia Jenks Bloomer (see above); and peromelia is a congenital absence or malformation of the extremities (the "melia" part, no doubt, links it to Earhart).

I have to admit this is indeed information. I can feel it rattling around inside my head, where Henry Fielding, extremities malformed, shall now forever romp in bloomers over the rolling hills of Wales, buzzed by a seventeenth-century painter in a twin-engine Vega.

If you should be so mired in the pre-postindustrial past as to take a train somewhere, it will carry you for miles between the ghosts of factories. They were built for the ages, with the thick walls and solid craftsmanship of the late nineteenth century, and they haven't fallen down, nor have we found another use for them. Every windowpane, even the highest and smallest, is broken, but the buildings still stand, factory and warehouse and loading dock by the tracks, and still almost visible on the blackened bricks is the painted boast that once said "Making the world's finest . . ."

I was an impressionable child in the late Industrial Age. I considered those posters. I was proud of my country, that it made linoleum and cameras and toasters and radios and locomotives, and everywhere factory whistles sang of its self-sufficiency. I am trying to be equally proud of our information management, but deep down inside, I feel that anything produced without belching smoke must be flimsy goods indeed.

CLOTHESLINES

IN GOOD WEATHER I HANG MY LAUNDRY OUT TO DRY on a clothesline in the backyard. Visitors are startled by it, as if I had traded in my car on a buggy and a horse to pull it, but I like to look at it there. Not that there's anything intrinsically lovely in my shabby shirts and unraveling towels, but they represent accomplishment, however small and ordinary: I have done the wash. I am looking at the physical evidence of work. Not work mysteriously, with luck, recorded in electronic pulses somewhere in the unknowable bowels of the computer, but real work, tackled, hung forth, on display, visible.

Instead of popping the stuff into the convenient adjacent dryer, I lug a heavy basket up the basement steps and out onto the lawn. One by one I shake out the jeans and T-shirts and pillowcases and pin them on the line as my grandmother taught me to, back when I was a tagalong child. My mother had no use for domestic accomplishments except painting and carpentry, but Grandmother, otherwise a history teacher, took pleasure in her physical skills—pie crust, darning, knitting, gardening, ironing—and tried to pass them down to me. Hanging the sheets crooked was slovenly; their corners must be squarely aligned. Shirts were hung by their tails so that the sleeves fattened out with a breeze and gestured wildly over the lawn. Dishtowels, to save space, might be hung from a single corner, but everything else was stretched for maximum air flow and minimum wrinklage, from pin to pin, preferably the one-piece, knob-headed pin from which dolls and Christmas angels could be made, because the metal clip on the pinch-type pin might rust and leave a mark, or so my grandmother believed.

When I am finished I stand back as my grandmother did—as all women once did—to admire the fruits of my labor. It was a pleasant thing to see on a sunny Monday morning, all down along the backyards, pretty women with their arms all raised, pinning up the sheets and shirts, small children running through them to feel the clean wet slap on their faces. It was ritual. It was what corporations now call job satisfaction. The worst of housewifery was always its invisibility. The housewife polished her kitchen floor and dusted the knickknacks and made the beds and swept down the cobwebs, and nobody noticed. Her family took cleanliness and punctual meals for granted and nobody else, unless specially invited, could see how hard she worked. Aside from the moist and shapely cake carried to the church bake sale, only the laundry was open to the public. It made, as the fashion industry says, a statement. Look, it said, I have been up since dawn; I have washed all these things and hung them forth clean and straight in the eyes of the world.

It was mildly competitive. Earlier was better than later, and she whose washing was first on the line was a better person than the sloven who didn't get it out till noon. Domestic linens in those days tended to be white, and the woman whose sheets were splotched and yellowish was a disgrace in the public eye. After the arrival of commercial washing products, advertisers lashed housewives on to orgies of whiteness. Laundry supplies crowded the grocery shelves and the airwaves, sponsoring afternoon radio dramas thenceforward known as soap operas. "Rinso white! Rinso white!" they warbled. "Happy little washday song!" The smell of Clorox hovered in the Monday morning air and something called "blueing" was put in the rinse water to conquer yellowing.

Clothesline replaced the hedges, rocks, and bushes on which linens had once been spread out to bleach and dry in the sunshine, and occasionally to blow into the neighbors' pigsty. Apparently it took an amazingly long time to invent, but once it arrived, it was a great improvement, and so were the clothespins that kept the clothes in place. Clothespins were whittled by hand, another physical art. Men who felt at ease only while doing something with their hands spent their leisure with a good small knife, piling up shavings between their feet, shaping small useful household objects or maybe just whittling the wood down to nothing for the pure relaxation of it, then choosing another piece to pare.

Long after washing machines took the backache out

of Mondays, clothesline lived on. Extra clothesline had many uses. Bad children could tie their sister to a tree with it and wait to see if the wolves would come to eat her. If you built a treehouse, clothesline was how you hauled up your supplies. Before bungee cords, it was used to tie large objects to the top of your car. You could fasten tomatoes to their stakes with it, or hold up your pants if your belt broke, or harness the dog to a wagon, or pull a child on a sled. It was the duct tape of its day.

Its day is done. The family laundry swaying in the morning sunlight, once a woman's weekly pride, is now a public confession of poverty. Clothes drying openly are seen in the blighted slums, line strung from windowsill to fire escape, and in the bleakest hardscrabble countryside behind a farmhouse needing paint. All but the most abject failures hide their laundry in a dryer. The walls of our houses have drawn a brick curtain over the triumphs and failures of housekeeping, which is anyway no longer the sole measure of a woman's worth.

The machine does it. The machine rose up in the nineteenth century and changed everything. It set us free from back-breaking, life-shortening work in the fields or bent over a washtub or a loom or a butter churn. It made life easier. Then it made life more comfortable, with the furnace, the elevator, cars, tractors, water heaters, electric lights. Then, at the end of the twentieth century, it went berserk. Unable to stop itself, it made life convenient to the point of atrophy, to what John Muir, naturalist and father of our national parks, called "the deadly apathy of luxury."

We no longer need to cash a check, mail a letter, wash the dishes, clean the cat's litter pan, learn to spell or multiply or cook, dial a phone number, vacuum the swimming pool, fold the clean diapers, rake the leaves, wind the clock, or move more than a fingertip to raise the room temperature or turn on the lights with our all-purpose remote controls. At Thanksgiving, when American families traditionally gather to watch football, nobody needs to get up to baste the self-basting turkey. And remember what a nuisance it was to read books, having to turn all those pages? Now we can plug the tape into the tape player and use nothing but our ears, hands free to scratch where it itches or pick at our cuticles. Driving, we needn't shift gears, crank down the windows, lock the doors, or put our foot on the gas pedal to keep up with traffic. Already we can punch our destination into a car and it will drive us there, avoiding collisions, while we whack at our laptops or take a nap in the backseat. Perhaps we can even send it to pick up the children at day care.

All this is wonderful news for paraplegics, but what of the rest of us? We might as well not have hands at all, those fabulously clever machines with which we climbed to the top of the food chain. For the time being, we still need them to click the mouse button, but that too is on the way out, they say, and soon we can lie on the couch and tell the computer what to do: "Fetch the sales chart for April 1994 and E-mail it to Branson. Oh, and while you're at it, tell him he's fired."

Life has never been more convenient. Our last remaining inconvenience is the rush-hour traffic jam that leaves us toxic with rage and frustration in a way that raking leaves and ironing shirts never did. Otherwise, life may be so easy it can scarcely be called life at all.

If we could contact our grandfathers and tell them we

no longer need to rise from our chairs to answer the phone or change the television channel, would they rejoice in our newfound happiness? Or fear we must be a generation of zombies, poleaxed with boredom?

Is it possible that all those fiddling little inconveniences like standing in line at the bank, licking postage stamps, and winding the clock kept us engaged with our days? At least we could look back on them at nightfall and know what we'd done, like the good housewife gazing at her laundry or the geezer with a row of smoothly sanded clothespins. Now, what we've done is invisible. All we've really achieved is a paycheck, which leads us to greatly exaggerate its importance, comparing its size to the size of our neighbor's, sacrificing all else on its altar, moving our families from state to state to follow its star. And even this one accomplishment we rarely get to fondle or even look at; it's been transferred electronically, and will show up by magic on the bank balance. Otherwise, even the longest meeting we sat through has vanished without a trace, and the rest is, we hope, somewhere on the C drive.

At Christmastime, we can order a fully decorated tree delivered to our home, and under it are the presents chosen by our "personal shopper," to whom we have faxed a brief description of our children, mates, and other loved ones, along with how much we're willing to spend on them. A professional wrapper at the store has wrapped them gaily, and our children's new toys will be as great a surprise to us as to them.

To be is to do. Since we can't see anything we've done, do we feel as if we don't much matter, even to ourselves? Not having left any imprint on the day's face, perhaps we weren't really there at all.

Therefore does the overpaid executive, when he can get home before dark, change his clothes and take out his lawn mower and, riding high and making a great noise, mow his lawn. Next year he'll probably get one of the new self-steering mowers that do the job unsupervised, but for now, when he's finished, he pauses for a moment to admire the green flatness and symmetry he has wrought with his own efforts, visible to the world. Therefore on the first warm day of spring do I hang my clothes on the line to dry in the sun, and pause for a moment to admire the fruits of my labor. When I bring them in, they smell good.

HEROES

WE USED TO HAVE HEROES. THEY COMMITTED BRAVE or marvelous deeds, and came home, and there was a parade. The father took the kid to the parade and boosted him up onto his shoulder and said, "Look, son! See that man on the white horse? That's Julius Caesar!" Or Lucky Lindbergh or Charles de Gaulle or Babe Ruth or Genghis Khan or whoever.

Heroes were good for us. The little boy on his father's shoulder may not have believed he would actually grow up to be Napoleon Bonaparte, but he sucked in a sense of the grander possibilities of life. Not scholarship, alas; no parades were mustered for philosophers, but then neither were roses and confetti thrown at those who had merely made a lot of money. Parade-worthiness called for courage, skill, vision, success, and virtue.

Heroes were men, because heroism meant action outdoors, climbing Everest, winning wars, galloping off with rescued maidens, all unsuitable for the gentler sex.

103

Men and women alike are uncomfortable with women in action. Nobody wants to know about Queen Boadicea leading her troops into battle, or about that English girl whose name I've forgotten—a lighthouse keeper's daughter, maybe—who rescued all those people from a sinking ship, rowing a small boat through wallowing seas. American girls have long been urged to admire the courage of Betsy Ross, a Philadelphia seamstress who was given a pattern and asked to run up a prototype flag for the rebellious colonies, and did. Women who made trouble, like Harriet Tubman and Clara Barton, were always unsuitable; what deeds a woman does should be done indoors, sitting down. Watching the parade, probably through a window, girls could dream only of marrying heroes, and heroes make terrible husbands.

Still, their glory shone over all. During the space of his hour in the sun, the hero was perfect. If he had flaws, if he beat his wife or picked his teeth, nobody wanted to know. The thought of him was nourishing and stimulating and broadened the heart's horizons, and nobody wanted to snatch back the curtain and expose the worm within. It would have been worth your life to point out that George Washington, worshiped as "the Moses of his country," bled the treasury during the Revolutionary War with enormous bills for his personal comforts while his troops went hungry. Nobody sneered that Teddy Roosevelt, glorious hero of the Battle of San Juan Hill, had missed the fight entirely by getting lost, and watched the whole thing from a nearby but unembattled hill. Debunking is a recent passion.

Is it envy? Do we all want to ride the white horse? Or have our hearts been honeycombed by cynicism? As soon as a hero arrives, we send reporters to pick through his household trash. In college, did he smoke pot? Cheat on exams? Did he tell us a lie? Who was that woman we saw him with? Who paid for the white horse? One by one they topple over into the muddy seas of sex and money roiling around their knees, and even prospective saint Mother Theresa was debunked before her body was cold, exposed as a grandstanding autocrat with no respect for local religions. Sports stars get watched with extra vigilance because, we tell each other, they are our children's role models; as a sports star behaves, so will our offspring. Apparently an entire generation plans to find fame and fortune dropping a ball through a hoop, which must make the future look bleak indeed for the short.

As of this writing, our most durable recent hero is Colin Powell, chairman of the Joint Chiefs of Staff during a brief war in the Persian Gulf in the early '90s. Military heroes have lost some of their glow now that they've put away their swords. No more Horatio Nelson aboard the *Victory*, Victory-o; no more "Look, there is Jackson standing like a stone wall. Rally behind the Virginians!" Heroes now view the battle on radar and transmit heroic instructions electronically from headquarters. Still, as long as we more or less won the war, the man in charge deserves to be a hero.

Years after the Gulf War, Powell remained a hero. On the Internet, fans wept and lamented, claiming that he had been the country's last and only hope, and without him we are surely doomed. Polls showed that if he changed his mind at any time about running for president, he could beat any other candidate including Abraham Lincoln. He seems an odd choice for a hero, though by all accounts a thoroughly nice man with an unimpeachable, probable reporter-proof, home life. He is black, or at any rate mocha, and more than half of all white Americans want him to be president, though considerably fewer blacks do; perhaps we feel that if we elect a black president we can finally put all this annoying guilt problem behind us. However, he was very clear about not being president, and his wife was even clearer, and presently he will fade away and leave us heroless again.

Being chronically dissatisfied with what we're offered, we might fare better if we simply invented our heroes. The Greeks did, and they were so satisfying that the Romans stole them and changed their names and made them Roman. The whole swarm of mythology's gods and goddesses provided the world with terrific stories and exciting characters and even the women could hold up their heads in the presence of Athena, goddess of wisdom, and Diana the huntress, who makes Diana the princess look like a Barbie doll. Unfortunately for our modern purposes, the gods and goddesses were not good. Their set lives were wildly inventive, sometimes involving birds and animals. Marital fidelity never crossed their minds, nor did diligent labor. Some of them drank heavily and, to judge from their statues and portraits, all of them habitually went around stark naked. Raw power, not virtue, made them heroes. If they wanted you to win the battle you won it; otherwise you got lunched. If you dissed them, they could change you into a cow or a plant before you could say knife. This undemocratic lifestyle would never play in twenty-first-century America.

We do, however, have the making of heroes at our fingertips now. I have a modest proposal to make, and the technology is already up and running.

We can create a virtual national hero. An interactive hero. We can lay his initial foundations with a mix of, say, Robin Hood, Batman, Bill Gates, Ronald Reagan,

Tiger Woods, and Robert E. Lee. Then we can start adjusting. On the hero's interactive Web site, polls will be taken every fifteen minutes, with respondents inputting preferences for his opinion on everything from handgun laws to animal rights. Trends will adjust our hero's noble visage according to current fashions in hairstyles, chins, and noses. Nobody will need to wait for the parade; the hero can be accessed twenty-four hours a day, and each time we check in with him he will have altered subtly, reflecting changes in the national climate. Have we wearied of the sensitive wimp who changes diapers? A sword appears in his hand and a Hemingway beard on his cheeks. Have we come to prefer cats to dogs? His loyal retriever is replaced by a tiger-cat or perhaps, in times of national belligerence, a tiger. Is the environment passé? He will stop recycling and clear-cut a national forest. His deeds, past and present, will be updated all through the day and night.

Women will finally come into their rights and have a hero of their own, starting with a mix of Katharine Hepburn and Betty Crocker, and she too will be adjusted, gaining or losing weight, flying fighter planes, or stirring the soup as molded by the polling process.

No more need we dread the exposure of a beloved public figure as an adulterous flimflam artist. Our heroes will be permanent. Everyone will love them, reflecting as they do our very selves. The nation will smile again. Should we feel downhearted, we can punch on the computer and bask in the restorative virtual presence of the perfect hero.

In fact, I can think of absolutely no reason why we couldn't elect him president. Nothing in the Constitution rules out an electronic leader. Free of the acrimony and noise of old-fashioned election campaigns, we can simply press "enter" on the keyboard and, without a dissenting vote to mar the occasion, watch him take the oath of office.

Then we can settle down at our desks to fine-tune his foreign policies and lower our taxes. Pure democracy, unsullied by human frailties, will at last be a reality, or at least a virtual reality, and all of us shall ride the white horse together, our voices raised in a mighty cheer of praise.

ART

FOR THE FIRST TIME IN SIX OR SEVEN THOUSAND YEARS, many people of goodwill find themselves confused about art. They want to enjoy it because enjoying art is something they expect of themselves as civilized persons, but they're unsure how to do so. They aren't even sure which of the visible objects are art and which are furniture, clothing, hors d'oeuvres, or construction rubble, and whether a pile of dead and decomposing rats is deliberate art or just another pile of decomposing rats.

They admire performance art and installation art, but can't figure out how to take it home and put it in the living room, so museums buy it, and face problems of their own. The artist, for instance, who sits at a table kneading raw dough and hypnotically chewing on pieces of it: suppose she comes down with indigestion, or has other plans for the day? The table remains, but without her, is it still art? How can you tell?

To clear up the confusion, the *New York Times* recently cornered a sampling of art professionals and demanded a definitive definition, which I shall pass on as a public service.

Art critic Robert Hughes said, "Something is a work of art if it is made with the declared intention to be a work of art and placed in a context where it is seen as a work of art."

Professor Thomas McEvilley said, "It is art if it is called art, written about in an art magazine, exhibited by a museum, or bought by a private collector."

Artist Jenny Holzer said, "I think you can rely on the artist's representation. He or she would have no reason to lie."

Art critic Arthur Danto said, "You can't say something's art or not art anymore. That's all finished."

Republican congressman Peter Hoekstra said, "Art is whatever people want to perceive it to be, but that doesn't mean the Federal Government should fund it."

Artist Alexander Melamid said, "We see art as fun. As long as it gives us some kick, it goes."

Artist Louise Bourgeois said, "Something is a work of art when it has fulfilled its role as therapy for the artist. I don't care about the audience."

I hope that clears it up. In short, if it has been hauled into a gallery or parked in front of a museum, it's art. Whatever people make while saying they're making art is art. If making it made them feel good, it is good art—though this doesn't help the passerby to distinguish it from the hors d'oeuvres. If people enjoy photocopying their genitalia or gluing teddy bears to the wall or wrapping bridges in toilet paper, it is art. What the beholder enjoys is his oven problem. Selah.

WORRIES

IN THE 1930S THERE WAS THE GREAT DEPRESSION AND people worried about freezing and starving to death. This was immediately followed by World War II, and people worried that the wrong people might win it. This was a big, serious war, not one of your tribal uprisings or turf squabbles that go by the name these days, and losing it would have been most unfortunate, and for a year or so there it looked entirely possible. We scanned the skies for planes, hoping they were ours; we held air-raid drills.

Reassuringly, we did win, but victory was immediately followed by the Cold War and the shadow of the Bomb.

Several generations grew up waiting for nuclear annihilation. Young couples mulled earnestly over whether it was morally wrong to have a baby, knowing its life would be so brief and its end so nasty. For a while we were told there would be some survivors, though they wouldn't feel very well; the official phrase on authoritative lips was, "The living will envy the dead." A handful of people moved to places like Montana where they thought they'd be out of harm's way. Suburbanites with backyards dug bomb shelters and stocked them with canned goods and bottled water, and a spirited public debate grew over whether, if your neighbors tried to squeeze in there with you, it was socially acceptable to shoot them.

The government issued instructions, freely available in every post office: we should unplug the toaster before a nuclear attack and hose the radiation off the roof afterward, take the children down to the basement, and avoid looking directly at the actual explosion because it might be bad for our eyes. As the bombs kept getting bigger, the instructions grew stranger. Those who lived in the cities and nearby suburbs should keep their gas tanks full at all times and be ready to jump simultaneously into their cars at the signal and drive to a designated outer suburb, after which they were on their own. Before fleeing the target cities, however, everyone should stop off to leave a forwarding address with his or her local post office.

Even the cheeriest citizens began to laugh hollowly.

Then we were told about "nuclear winter," and it seemed there wouldn't be any survivors, not even sickly ones, not even in Montana, and nobody would need a toaster or a forwarding address. The inevitable nuclear war was going to mean the end, not just of civilization as we knew it, but of all life on earth, which could really give you something to cry about. Parents had been in the habit of telling their children, "Don't make such a fuss, it's not the end of the world." Now it was. Any day now.

Then mysteriously, almost overnight, without our nudging it, the whole structure of fear began to fall apart like a computerized film of a stone castle coming apart silently, a chunk at a time, battlement and tower and drawbridge breaking off and slipping down pulverized into the moat.

We looked around us and found nothing to worry about. The economy with all its ups and downs was ticking along; the evil Russian empire was a handful of quarrelsome clans; the thundercloud of communism shriveled down to a cranky old fellow with a beard on an island off Florida. Nobody had ever been so safe or

111

so rich as we, so qualified to dance rejoicing naked in the streets and take up painting, philosophy, botany, and orgies.

Alas, we'd forgotten how. Safety had been so long ago, somewhere back in the summer of 1929, that nobody remembered what to do with it, and a nameless dread struck terror into our hearts: there must be something to worry about, but what? Since nothing's in sight, the peril is invisible, much the most worrying kind of peril. We scrambled to lay hands on it, and found it everywhere.

Previously unnoticed threats to our personal health and safety sprang up, and the more we brooded about them, the more precious and endangered we seemed to ourselves.

All through the Great Depression, the worldwide war, and the danger of nuclear winter, personal health was a simple matter. Eat something from each of the four basic food groups. Get some exercise and fresh air. Brush your teeth. Wash your hands before meals. Sleep eight hours a night. Don't masturbate, or at least not constantly. Have a bath and a bowel movement daily, and greet the world whistling, all obligations to the flesh fulfilled.

Under the new scrutiny, the rules swelled and subdivided and exploded beyond our ability to memorize them. The four food groups multiplied into thousands, divided unevenly into those that would help us live forever and the much larger group that would end up killing us. As soon as we thought we understood, those in charge reshuffled the categories. Day before yesterday alcohol was poison, yesterday a couple of drinks improved the heart, today they'll be the death of us. Tuesday eggs were the staff of life; Wednesday they were lethal; Thursday they're back on the menu. Last week we were to live on complex carbohydrates; this week, nothing but fruits and vegetables, but alack! They're covered with carcinogenic pesticides. Every silver lining has its cloud. Do selenium pills prevent cancer or cause it? Does running five miles a day prevent or cause heart attacks, and what are the odds on getting hit by a car, and will its driver be saved or killed by the air bag?

Where once we learned to live with a single major worry, we now run distracted along a smorgasbord of thousands. Recently I managed to break into a bottle of vitamin pills (how much is enough? How much is too much?) and my eye fell on the warning message. The wad of cotton that they pack into the top, either to keep the pills from rattling or to persuade us there are twice as many in the bottle, must be discarded at once. Not because I might eat it and choke, though there's that too, but because if I leave it there, as time goes by I'll keep opening the bottle (squeezing flanges together, pressing down while turning) and the cotton will become contaminated with bacteria. From where? Why, from the air I keep letting into the bottle, the same air I am recklessly breathing, the same air that is even now settling over my coffee cup.

An ad in the *New York Times* shouts rudely at me, "WARNING—YOUR TOOTHBRUSH IS CONTAMINATED." It seems that my toothbrush, exposed, is soaking up "millions of airborne microorganisms that would normally be injected into your bloodstream via your gums." However, for eighty dollars plus shipping and handling, I can buy a cabinet for my toothbrush that will bombard it with ultraviolet rays, killing ninety-nine percent of my invisible enemies.

I have no idea what ultraviolet rays do when injected into my bloodstream via my gums, and I don't plan to find out. I remember when people who thought germs were nesting in their toothbrushes got slammed into psychotherapy.

When we buy an appliance, we can't find the operating instructions imbedded in the warnings: we are not to thrust our bare hands into the blender while it's blending, nor into the toaster while it's toasting. When I went to install a new cat-hair filter in the air cleaner, I was arrested by the plastic bag it came in, stamped every two inches in red ink with a warning and then, for good measure, the same warning, also in red, on stickers pasted all over both sides: DANGER—IMPORTANT NOTICE. REMOVE FILTER FROM PLASTIC BAG. BEFORE USE DESTROY BAG COMPLETELY. All right, all right. I had been in the habit of recycling plastic bags but this one's a killer. Unless disarmed before I install the filter, it will spring up howling and plaster itself over my mouth and nose. Plastic doesn't burn very well, so it will have to be scissors, but plastic is clumsy to cut and how small must the pieces be before it's "destroyed completely"?

The warning is repeated forty or fifty times in French, and I see that the French, more relaxed than Americans, recommend its destruction *"après usage."* In France, then, I could put the filter in first, before turning my attention to the deadly bag. Ah, those reckless, daredevil foreigners, they'll be sorry.

In America, hazards lurk in every corner of our happy homes. Bed, once a haven, is another war zone, populated as it is with millions of dust mites and their droppings. Considered as companion animals, they're no problem and don't require feeding, since they live on

114

flakes of dead skin. My dead skin. Their drawback, apart from invisibility, is that they can't be toilet-trained. My mattress and pillows are their litter pan, and the whole mess is highly allergenic, and small wonder, but for ninety dollars I can get covers that will keep them contained inside the zoo on which I sleep. I assume they've been around for millennia, but nobody worried about them before, and I'm terribly sorry they've told me now.

My mother, whose college days were spent learning silly songs, used to sing,

Bar the door, they're a-comin' through the windows,
Bar the windows, they're a-comin' through the door.
Holy Christ, they're a-comin' down the chimney,
Judas priest, they're a-comin' through the floor.

Shadowy assassins will break into our aspirin and lace it with cyanide. Children we have never seen before will figure out how to press down while turning and drink our paint thinner; their parents will sue. Unheralded sources of cholesterol will colonize our blood vessels and prevent us from living forever. A man on the opposite street corner, waiting for the light to change, will fire up a cigarette and the smoke will drift toward us on a stray current of wind, sealing our doom. Did we wash our hands with soap for the full thirty seconds after touching raw chicken? Have we gathered the family for a fire drill this week? Are we wearing government-approved sunglasses? Last spring two people wished me a safe Easter. Safe from what? Exploding eggs? Rabid rabbits?

In Paducah, Kentucky, the mayor has sworn a solemn vow to tear down all the old buildings in town, lest neighborhood children break into them and fall down the stairs. Not that this has ever happened, but you never can tell. In the three years between 1995 and 1997, he bulldozed 366 historic structures, ignoring the preservation ordinance and outraging history-minded citizens. When attacked, he replied, "The primary goal of government is the protection of public safety. Anything else is just extra."

Where once relative health and relative safety were sufficient, we now demand absolute, permanent health and utter safety against the remotest contingency. Lighting a candle the other day, I considered the box of kitchen matches. In the usual large red capitals it warned me, "CAUTION! DO NOT DROP." Satan tempted me, and I fell. Looking around to make sure I was unobserved, I let go of the box. It hit the floor. The matches rattled slightly and lay still. I had called their bluff.

Perhaps a secondary danger lurks in this business of warning us against everything: how are we to know what might, just possibly, be really dangerous? When they tell us the dam has broken, the city is on fire, the plague is sweeping toward us, will we flee? Or change channels? Can we still distinguish between a kitchen match and a tornado?

He who has reached the end of the American rainbow and acquired pots of gold and a house full of possessions can worry about their safety as well as his own. Imprisoned behind alarms and bars and surveillance cameras, the man who once had nightmares about sniper fire and land mines has nightmares about miscreants making off with his electronic devices. Once he has all the protective equipment in place, he can fret about faraway hackers breaking into his computer and reading his deleted E-mail, or into his answering service and learning that his wife's meeting ran late and she won't be home till seven.

An article in a popular magazine reminds me sternly that the paper shredder is my most important household appliance. Unless I shred all my trash, bad people will join the raccoons in picking through my coffee grounds and cat-food cans, and find a receipt with my credit card number on it, and use it nefariously. As soon as the trash is shredded, I can settle down to worrying about alien abductions, CIA plots, and the Trilateral Commission.

If I had children around, I should want not for worries. Those who produce a child open Pandora's own box of perils.

Never in the history of the world have there been such safe children as our middle-class young. Wolves will not eat them, neither shall we lose half of them in the first year to infant diarrhea nor the survivors in their teens to tuberculosis, smallpox, or polio. Laws protect them from endangering their futures with beer and cigarettes as their parents did; V-chips protect them from seeing smut on television as their parents do. Supervisors make sure their safety helmets are buckled on before they touch a soccer ball. Cribs are wired with sound systems so parents in another room can detect the faintest whimper. Baby strollers, once flimsy folding contraptions of struts and canvas, have ballooned into massive armored vehicles ready to take on a charging rhinoceros. Furniture is made with special padding so toddlers bump not their heads. Every few months the government issues new regulations on children's car seats and new penalties for those who didn't hear about them. A friend has recently installed new windows in

117

her house, and each window displays a large, nondetachable tag saying, "WARNING! Screens will not stop a child from falling out window. Open top window only!"

Children are no longer allowed outdoors unsupervised. "It's too dangerous," their parents assure me. If I ask why, they shake their heads and say, "It's not like it used to be." Danger is nonspecific now, and invisible, and everywhere.

My old stove died and I bought a new one. Strong men came and delivered it, pushing it into place with many an oath and grunt. When it was installed, there were pieces left over, a sort of steel brace contraption and some bolts. "That's the antitilt mechanism," explained the stalwart gent. "Like, if a kid bounces up and down on one end of the stove, it won't fall over on him." Considering the bulk and weight of the thing, it would need to be an enormous kid, well over two hundred pounds, and mighty determined. Somehow it seemed unlikely. Much more likely, the kid simply stuffs a sibling into the oven and turns it on to broil. Apparently our guardians haven't thought of this yet, but when they do they'll fix it so I can no longer open the oven or turn it on.

Not so long ago, it was thought that healthy, active children were going to hurt themselves and learn by the experience; if Sally climbed a tree and fell out of it, she'd be more careful next time. Assessing risks was part of growing. Even mothers were heard to say, "Don't be such a sissy." In the backyards and playgrounds, "scaredy-cat" and "chicken" were on everyone's lips and called for immediate action to restore what the duelists of old would have called our honor. We dared each other to jump off the wall, climb out on the roof, eat a caterpillar, dive into the quarry, smoke a cigarette, ring doorbells and run, and ride no-hands down the steepest hills. To refuse a dare was to be scorned eternally. Our courage was tested daily, courage back then being an essential virtue, now replaced by caution. Is it possible that our children, warned and shielded from birth, will grow into anxious, gray-spirited wimps? Or maybe they'll all rebel and go skydiving off Everest.

All through human history, up until now, facing the risks of living without whimpering or cowering was a mark of character. Courage had snob appeal; the upper classes felt themselves braver than the underlings, and punished their children for cowardice. When there were no risks in the immediate area, they buckled on their armor and rode off to look for some. What sort of mice have we become, then, that we're afraid of our toothbrushes?

It's insidious, this habit of worrying so much about so little, and it grows on us. It's undignified. It ill becomes a gallant and spirited nation to frighten itself with the pinpricks of daily life.

Probably it's too late to go back to worrying about Hitler, but surely we can find something with more stature than accidentally smothering ourselves in a plastic bag. There must be some desperate danger out there. Let us search it out, something solid to cry about, and if we can't find it, well, we might just give over the habit entirely. It's probably a health hazard anyway.

DESKS

THE COMPUTER, WITH ITS ATTENDANT PRINTER, monitor, keyboard, and mouse pad, sprawls over what used to be my desk. I do my actual work at what used to be the dinner table, which the Internal Revenue Service doesn't consider part of my office because sometimes I eat on it, scraping papers aside to make room for a plate. This is depressing, since a desk is expected to be a seething wallow of books and notes and folders, half-empty coffee cups, jugs of pens and pencils, torn envelopes, peanut shells, and unpaid bills, all topped with a sleeping cat, but a dinner table is not. Working at the dinner table, I feel disorganized and apologetic. However, my desk no longer has room to lay down even a single sheet of paper, let alone prop my chin on my elbows in the time-honored posture of thought, and there's no place for the cat except on top of the monitor, blocking the air vents. A typewriter could share the desk with me, perched modestly in its own space, but a computer needs it all. Actually, the computer has replaced the desk, leaving only its legs sticking out below. Sometimes I think about reclaiming it by moving the computer to the dinner table and using the mouse pad as a place mat, but who wants to dine face-to-face with a Pentium tower?

The office desk once had room to assemble a creative mess, and the mess's nature and depth proclaimed your occupation and identity; your labors were spread forth for the world to see. Now everyone's computer looks alike and everyone's accomplishment is hidden inside it. At the office where I sometimes work, the computer has its own form-fitting surface and the desk is a molded plastic shelf the width of a coffee cup and half a sandwich. The corporate world has discovered that it can cram more workers into the given space if they no longer have desks. Proper desks, with drawers. The floors in the communal area are mounded with toppling piles of paper. Occasionally a memo appears on the screen ordering us to dispose of these piles, but some of them are indispensable and the rest are quickly replaced. Some advanced techno offices have abolished the whole concept of privately claimed space, and employees wander nomadically among differently talented computers, adjusting the chair heights as they browse from space to space, and then try to remember beside which mouse pad they left their lunch.

It's all very democratic. The boss still has a private office with a door to close, but no more elbow room than I do. Once, you knew the boss was the boss by the sheer acreage of his polished mahogany surface, supporting only a marble inkstand and a studio portrait of his wife; papers cluttered the lesser desks of the lesser workers but the boss was there for his bossly qualities, not for his paperwork, and he maintained his authority by the great expanse of wood that separated him from the lowly worms he summoned. Now, so have the mighty fallen, his computer is just as ugly as mine and his elbows just as cramped. Who can respect a man who works on a plastic shelf?

The very word "desk" has taken on an almost Dickensian fustiness. We have "work stations" now, always in the same mind-numbing beige as the computer and its adjuncts. We are too modern for desks, and have no need for old-fashioned printed dictionaries or paper or pens, no need even for a telephone, since we're all connected by fax and E-mail. Should we, for some reason, need to think, we can go out and sit in the car and think. Should we want to write about nightingales and enchanted princes, I don't know where we'd go. The neighborhood tavern maybe.

Sometimes I wander or take guided tours through the restored houses of the eighteenth and nineteenth century and gaze longingly at the desks. The desk of the man of the house was a wonder of solidity. On a plantation it might have been fashioned of a single plank from one of his mightiest oaks, slain for the purpose. Always it spoke of responsibility. Of permanence. Of plats and deeds, wills and investments, and a thousand letters written to lawyers, newspaper editors, friends, congressmen, and erring sons. Here he did his accounts and kept his journal, recording crops, weather, politics, and appointments. The desk of the lady of the house was a pretty thing, every hinge and handle twinkling in brass, with dozens of small drawers and cubbyholes. It spoke of a thousand letters written to mother and sisters and married daughters; of recipes, menus, invitations, lists, thank-you notes, announcements of births, deaths, and marriages, and a diary meticulously updated and locked with a tiny golden key.

When he sat at his desk he knew he was important and in charge here. When she sat at hers she knew she held the reins of her family's interconnections, household, and social position.

Writing on a desk was different from writing on a computer. It was more serious, a worthier occupation, because it was the desk's purpose. The computer was not designed for writing and produces it reluctantly, impatient to be about more suitable duties in Quattro or Quark, to collate a list or position clip art in a

122

newsletter. If we dally too long over the shape of a thought, it drums its fingers, clicks and buzzes, and then thrusts a screen saver into our faces. Professors everywhere complain that college papers have grown wondrously long, fattened on gobs of facts from the Internet, but contain no original thoughts or conclusions. The computer's knowledge is miles wide but only an inch deep, and it's always in a hurry. Original thoughts are gum on its shoe.

You cannot keep a diary on the computer because it so plainly doesn't care about your secret yearnings or when the first rose bloomed. It inhibits musing. It discourages philosophy. It scorns sentiment.

Our forebears wrote copiously on desks. Even the busiest man of affairs wrote thousands and thousands of letters. People kept them, because letters were felt to be important, and when the collection outgrew the desk drawers it was stored in trunks and boxes; love letters were traditionally tied up with ribbon. Later the letters of the important were published in thick leather volumes. Historians frolic through them. This is what makes our history so rich and flavorsome. We have, not just the Declaration of Independence, but what its authors thought while they were making it, which tavern they went to after work, and what vegetables Jefferson planted when he got home. We know, not just that the British burned Washington in 1814, but what the weather was like and how many people Dolley Madison was expecting for dinner (forty). Pity the scholars studying the thin dry history of our deskless days, after everyone has pressed Delete Message and Empty Trash Folder on our E-mail. Nothing will remain but official documents and what the reporters learned and the newspapers printed. History without food, rain, or parties, without sick children, doubts, misgivings, rheumatism, or rumination. History with no private life at all. No soul.

The desk encouraged soul. A person seated at a desk could concentrate with an intensity not possible while facing the fidgety computer screen, reach deeply into his vitals, and produce *À la Recherche du Temps Perdu,* sprinkling madeleine crumbs on his papers. A person could write "Ozymandias," *Origin of Species,* or "Shall I compare thee to a summer's day?" The desk even tolerated frivolity, and a person could write limericks on it, or *The Wind in the Willows,* without insulting its scientific workings. The computer will transmit the silliest of jokes via E-mail but it refuses to countenance *The Importance of Being Earnest.*

The polished rosewood or oaken plank or shabby leather-cornered blotter pad leaked its intellectual leisure up into the hand and heart, and never hustled the muse or the diary keeper or the letter writer. Neither did it break down regularly and need to be repaired at great expense, damaging the owner's self-esteem; neither did it require upgrading every two years at even greater expense. It was a place of quiet permanence in the life of the mind. A person could sit reading at a desk for hours, relaxed and attentive. Reading on a computer screen is a jittery business and few people can manage more than three paragraphs before clicking off to something new, which is just as well, since looking at the screen produces something called CVS, or Computer Vision Syndrome, leading to fatigue, a burning sensation, difficulty focusing, and headaches. There was no Desk Vision Syndrome.

All the pundits agree that the triumph of the computer has been an earthshaking revolution, but it might be changing us even more profoundly than we think. The computer is not only here to stay, it may already have taken us over, like the harmless-looking space parasites in a bad old movie. Already it may have hopelessly splintered our brains and trivialized our souls by gobbling the desks where we used to sit, propped on our elbows, and think.

NATURE

LAST SPRING MY FRIEND EILEEN OPENED HER DOOR TO a brace of badly frightened twelve-year-olds, one a neighbor's daughter, the other her classmate visiting for the afternoon. Alone in the house, they'd heard a noise in the kitchen and gone to look. It was a mouse, they stammered anxiously, a mouse running all over the place, and they'd fled out the other door and over to Eileen's, because they remembered her mentioning mice and mousetraps. They needed to borrow a mousetrap, fast.

Eileen dug out a couple of traps and decided, since the girls seemed so shaken, she should come along to supervise. They headed across the lawns, but the girls dragged their feet, reluctant to go back to that kitchen. "It's a *big* mouse," said one. "Mrs. Carlton? How big do mice get? Like this?" She held her hands a foot apart and Eileen's heart sank; nobody wants to cope with an outraged rat. "With, like, this great big scary tail," the other one added, shuddering reminiscently. "All fluffed up."

Boldly Eileen marched into the kitchen, sealed off the escape routes, found a broom, and escorted the panicked squirrel back outside.

These were twelve-year-olds of normal intelligence who attended an excellent school and lived in the kind of inconvenient green tree-lined suburb where parents these days raise their children. Presumably they had watched thousands of hours of television, including animal cartoons and Walt Disney. Mickey Mouse's is said to be the most recognized face in the world, and while he doesn't look much like a mouse, he looks even less like a squirrel. And suburbs being what they are, this can hardly have been the first flesh-and-blood squirrel to cross the girls' path. It was just the first they'd noticed. The first that mattered, being in the kitchen instead of out in the great blur beyond its walls.

In another suburb, several years ago, a friend and I leaned against the friend's car chatting. This friend was in her thirties and held a doctoral degree in agricultural science; she was raised in suburban Connecticut and had lived all her life in the East, mostly in suburbs. As we talked, she picked up a small rounded object from the hood of her car and turned it over and over in her fingers. "Isn't this a funny-looking thing?" she said. "What do you suppose it can be?"

I thought this was a joke of sorts, and smiled, but she continued to puzzle over her find. "It's an acorn," I offered at last. "They come from oak trees. You're parked under an oak tree." The same oak she'd been parking under for four years, every day getting out of her car and crunching acorns underfoot on the sidewalk.

"Really?" she said. "Is that what they look like?" She considered it another moment and then tossed it away. She wasn't in the least embarrassed.

And last winter a nice young couple came to visit me on my mountain. My feeder was besieged with birds, and presently, bored, the young wife glanced out the window at them. "Look, dear," she said to her husband. "There's a robin."

What doomed vagabond was this, a robin in February, poor thing, with the snow so deep on the ground? I jumped up to look and there under the feeder, blazing red, hopped the official bird of the woman's home state as well as of mine. "Cardinal," I said, but she had already turned away. In her hometown the spring lawns are littered with robins, but she said, "I don't know much about birds," as one who says, "I don't understand fiber optics."

Most good people speak highly of Nature. You can hear the capital *N* in their voices and see the vague green poster in their minds. They approve of national parks where those so minded can go visit it, and deplore the loss of rain forests that might have concealed a cure for human cancer. They also refer to the "environment," but more cautiously, since this means something quite different, a highly charged political contention involving how mane trees to sell off and how much industrial waste to let into the rivers. The environment concerns human incomes, human health, human elections. Nature, on the other hand, is everything that doesn't concern us. Everything out there that isn't ours.

Looking back, the great taxonomists of the eighteenth and nineteenth centuries seem unwholesomely obsessed. What demonic urge sent them into the jungles and deserts collecting and classifying such useless leaves and hugs? Why did it absorb their lives and make them so happy; why did they rejoice at having their names attached forever to small brown spiders? Look at Sir Joseph Banks, home from Cook's voyage to the South Seas, the ship wallowing under bottles and jars of specimens, cases of leaves and berries and worms, enough to keep him joyfully examining and naming the rest of his days. Why did it once seem to matter that a brownish gray moth at the window wasn't just a moth, but a moth of the family Lithosiidae, and not only that but of the genus *Crambidia,* but different from other Crambidiae, with a name of its own, *Crambidia pallida* Packard, having once made someone named Packard— maybe just an ordinary boob like us, poking around with a flashlight—very happy to have spotted it?

Here on the mountain, I find myself sounding educational with guests: that's a tulip polar, an eastern chickadee, a yellow swallowtail, a wild aster. Older guests at least feign attention, but the younger ones are openly skeptical. One man said, not unkindly, "How would *you* know?" He meant only that nobody was paying me to have learned such frippery, therefore why would I have done so, therefore why should he believe me? Nobody under forty will eat the roadside blackberries anymore, having only me to vouch for their character.

In truth, I don't know how I know. One autumn in elementary school, I remember, we all brought in assortments of fallen leaves and pressed them between sheets of waxed paper and labeled them: red maple, black locust, white birch. I think that was the limit of our formal instruction in country matters, but somehow there were things we just knew. Perhaps they seemed more important then, or perhaps information used to travel around loose in the air instead of being extracted from computers or purchased from adult-education classes, and perhaps we absorbed it through our skins, which may have been more porous then. Most of my contemporaries, however urbanized, can still tell a hawk from a handsaw without remembering how they learned; many of them in youth gathered and labeled collections of butterflies, or rocks, or seashells, and no one thought them peculiar. They would have been embarrassed, once, not to know what they were looking at outdoors. Now it is I who am embarrassed that I do know. The politely unspoken response to my information is "Get a life."

A few specialized observers linger, mostly trout fishermen and bird-watchers, though the bird-watchers aren't getting any younger, but the fact is that nature really doesn't matter anymore, even to the farmer. Well grounded in agriscience, farmers need to know only how much of which fertilizer per acre and what new hybrid corn resists his herbicides. If, in thirty years' time, the entire population goes to its grave unable to distinguish bats from butterflies, assuming either are still around, it won't make any difference at all. Linnaeus and Banks and Audubon might think they'd missed great joy in their lives, as if they'd lived in a house of a thousand rooms and never left the kitchen, but who misses what he's never known?

For a generation now, everything of any importance has concerned technology and the world outside its windows is withering away. The child who can't tell a squirrel from a mouse but can work a computer has a strong Darwinian edge over the child who can hoot like an owl and tell the delicious wild boletus mushroom from the deadly amanita, but can't surf the Net. Traits unnecessary for survival shrivel and drop away.

Visiting in another climate, I ask my host, "What kind of tree is that?"

"Tree?" He squints up at it, all leafy over his backyard, and shrugs. "That? Just a tree, I guess."

ELECTION NIGHT

IF SOMEONE REACHED DOWN AND TOOK AWAY OUR great American Fourth of July, an outcry would ensue. Someone or something, however, has snatched our great American election night from us, and hardly a murmur can be heard.

Once it was a glorious occasion, faster and more exciting than the World Series, as deeply rooted in the nation's life as Thanksgiving turkey; a night of nail-gnawing suspense, to be followed by a morning of relief and rejoicing or blackest despair. Parties were struck like sparks across the land. The faithful, who had rung so many phones and doorbells and passed out so many tracts, gathered at every local campaign headquarters and waited, laughing nervously and chilling the hopeful champagne. The county newspaper I work for always threw a party on the courthouse lawn across the street, with an enormous chalkboard on which to record the returns as they dribbled in. The whole county came, and with each fresh tally there was groaning or dancing. Parties often staggered on into the morning hours. Many remember the Kennedy-Nixon election of 1960 and how, when they finally turned off the radio, changed their clothes, and went to the office, it still wasn't over.

In some ways it was an occasion of divisiveness, and the children of Democrats and Republicans threw stones at each other for weeks in advance, but the citizens were split only in half instead of into our usual millions of shards. Within the parties there was brotherly love; all like-minded voters stood shoulder to shoulder against the enemy, at least for a week.

Politics was simpler then. Everyone was a Democrat or a Republican and proud of it, and knew exactly what it entailed: Democrats knew Republicans were mean and greedy; Republicans knew Democrats were soft in the head. Both voted the straight ticket, believing his hand would shrivel up if it touched the opposite lever, even for county sheriff; a child of the house who deserted the family allegiance was an outcast. Both parties felt the results meant life or death, the prince against the dragon, the white hats against the horse thieves, and the whole future of our country trembled in the balance all night long. (In olden times when tallies were carried around on horseback, the suspense went on for weeks; in the Adams-Jefferson election of 1796 they counted votes all winter, which makes for a grand long party.)

Everyone believed the outcome mattered. Up until about the mid-1970s, we felt that this democracy thing represented a choice of doors, one of which, if given a gentle push, would open onto a perfect society of peace on earth, lowered taxes, the widow and orphan fed, and the rest of us whistling the "Ode to Joy" as we bent to our profitable tasks. The other door led to ruin and chaos. It was exciting. People punched each other out in barrooms. Even when the result was a done deal, generations listened to the national party conventions on the radio, and the fine hairs on the backs of their necks rose up and quivered at the sonorous roll call and responses: "Mr. Chairman, the great state of Alabama . . ." This is hard to explain to the young, politics as a kind of proto-Super Bowl.

Election bets were laid. Due to the solemn nature of the occasion, many pledged a forfeit instead of vulgar cash, the loser to walk backward all day or push a raw

131

egg around the block with his nose. Many merry Wednesdays ensued.

Strange as it seems now, nobody knew the outcome in advance. In our early days, people guessed at it by the size of the crowds when the candidate spoke from a stump, and whether they were cheering or throwing vegetables. Early opinion polls were primitive: a reporter stood on a street corner and asked twenty people how they were going to vote. Being less accustomed then to media intrusion, seven of the twenty told him to stuff it. Armed with the thirteen, he went back to the newsroom and wrote that Dewey was a cinch to beat Truman.

Science has saved us from stressful uncertainty. Exquisitely calibrated polls are updated daily, even hourly; hundreds, maybe thousands of polls. They've done for elections what amniocentesis did for pregnancy—stolen the surprise. I have no idea how they're taken. I have never been asked, and I don't know anyone who has ever been asked, so it may be that they use some form of electronic surveillance that can see into the hearts of the voters and record their vacillations, so the candidates can adjust their positions accordingly. Or it may be done with a Ouija board, or astrological computations. Or it may be that the whole thing is a hoax and there are no polls, just results. The important thing is that voters and votees believe them, and by the weekend before the election the results are already in, polls having replaced votes. There's no pressing reason to hold an election at all now and we might as well cut straight to the inaugural balls, especially since there's no time for election-night parties anymore. After the long, slow buildup, the weary months of ads and speeches, charges and counter-

132

charges, the whole thing is over in an eye blink, and the West Coast complains that it scarcely has time to pull the lever.

Those in charge of broadcasting the event used to have a grand time all evening and into the night. The eyes of the world were upon them. Two sat at the desk, the rest were stationed around the country taking exit polls and talking to prospective mayors. Waves of results rolled across the country from east to west. The balance shifted. The tension mounted. Viewers and listeners sat spellbound; nobody touched that dial. Now, though they still allot the evening to coverage, they have little to do but traipse from headquarters to head-quarters, lugging cameras, interviewing victor and vanquished after the fact.

The fun is gone, but so is the passion that made it fun. Our tribal drama that filled the place once filled by heaven and hellfire, the visceral inherited tug-of-war between left and right that once defined us dissolved quite suddenly and left us empty-handed. Politicians no longer even call themselves Democrats or Republicans, for fear of offending someone, and make up labels like "moderate centrist" or "neoconservative," as if having no political convictions were the ultimate political virtue. Certainly this leaves them free to stand wherever the polls tell them to stand, and leaves their speechwriters free to ramble through family values and a nondenominational God, decorating them with metaphors like "a thousand points of light" and "morning in America" that for a minute, if held in the right light, seem to mean something important. The candidates all struggle to out-bland each other to the vanishing point. This is why so many people voted for Ross Perot in 1992: they remembered which one he was, the rich little gnome with the ears.

Half of us don't vote at all, let alone ring doorbells and pass out leaflets. Except for a handful of isolated passions—abortion, Hillary Clinton's hair—our public convictions have faded, and if neither of these bozos will actually lower my taxes, why bother?

Some pundits blame our apathy on selfishness. Others blame the deteriorating quality of the candidates and the sleaziness of their tactics; they point vaguely back into a golden past when seekers of public office were brave and noble, selfless and dedicated, and campaigned like honest gentleman.

In 1840, William Henry Harrison ran against the incumbent Matty Van Buren, who was a bit of a dandy; his enemies said he scented his fluffy sideburns with French cologne. His supporters retaliated by saying that all Harrison wanted in life was a log cabin, a jug of hard cider, and a pension. This was a peculiar thing to say about a country gentleman from a distinguished old Virginia family, but his handlers pounced on it like a duck on a june bug. They said Harrison was indeed a simple backwoodsman, unlike Van Buren the fop. They sang,

> Let Van from his coolers of silver drink wine And lounge on his cushioned settee.
> Our man on his buckeye bench can recline; Content with hard cider is he.

They plastered the country with posters of his log cabin birthplace and passed out log cabin badges and oceans of hard cider. It was great fun, and he won.

Now, I happen to have been to Harrison's birthplace, and if that's a log cabin I'm the Taj Mahal. A serene and stately brick Georgian mansion, it sits on many

134

thousands of fertile acres, its parklike gardens sloping down to the James River. It was built in 1726 by Benjamin Harrison IV, William Henry's grandfather, and all of our first ten presidents were guests there, though not simultaneously. They drank classier tipples than cider.

His neighbors must have had a good giggle over those posters.

Harrison's grandson Benjamin funded his successful 1888 campaign by selling Cabinet seats in advance to the highest bidder.

A pol was always a pol. There's no use blaming our modern candidates. We've simply let the fires go out. Politics, once our national passion, our all-American sport, bores us. Gone are the convivial local party clubs, where voters could take their troubles and parking tickets to their ward heeler, who fixed things up. Even on college campuses, political idealism looks as quaint as bell-bottoms. In the personal ads, the lonely specify their future love's height, weight, age, and hair color, but never politics; Karl Marx and Richard Nixon can stroll into the sunset hand in hand because it doesn't matter any more. Neither of the mystic doors will open onto a perfect world and no one will push an egg around the block with his nose.

Election night joins our yesterdays, and yet another excuse for an all-night party has dropped off the calendar.

FALLING IN LOVE

LAST SPRING THE *WASHINGTON POST* SENT A REPORTER and a photographer to cover the prom of my old high school. They found that tuxedos are still rented, dresses still agonized over, bow ties still assembled, and expensive products applied to the hair and skin for the grand occasion, just as in the olden days. The news was that fully half the celebrants came with friends and groups of friends of their own gender. Those with dates were offhand about them; they'd been chosen at the last minute from a pool of classmate possibilities. One girl had asked a boy who said yes and then changed his mind, claiming that he wanted to be fresh and rested for his SATs the next day. Another girl said she was relieved to have no date because, "You don't have any pressure with friends."

Six girls had clubbed together and rented a limousine, waiting happily for it while their mothers took pictures and videotapes of their flowering daughters decked in spring finery, unclaimed by blushing young men in tuxedos. Two boys, unable to scratch up a ride elsewhere, joined them for the elegant brief journey. In the limo, they all watched *Die Hard with a Vengeance* on the VCR while listening to Bone Thugs-N-Harmony on the C D player.

At the prom, girls danced with each other, or in clusters of half-a-dozen girls. Boys trolled the refreshments, joyfully unencumbered. "It's a special night," one explained to the reporter. "You want to be free to do whatever you want."

After the prom, those interviewed said the evening had been just as they'd hoped it would be.

I graduated from that school. I went to the prom, with orchids pinned to my chest, little cream-colored orchids with purple edging. My date was madly, helplessly, desperately in love with me. I too was in love, though with someone else, who loved another. We were all in love. The whole school. In love or in recovery, bruised

136

but brave, still carrying a torch, still writing terrible poetry and poking coins into the jukebox to endlessly replay the ballad we danced to last summer. The intensity of our passion was the measure of our worth, and he or she who loved but reasonably was a wingless soul, a poor spiritless clod.

Male and female alike, we dissected the nature of true love. It was understood that what we called "the real thing" would strike only once in a lifetime, and if it misfired or came to grief the rest of our days would be hardly worth living. Was it, this time, the real thing or only another chimera? Love at first sight—the French *coup de foudre,* or thunderbolt; the stranger across a crowded room; Cupid's blind arrow—was generally held to be the purest form because it was unswayed by any factors but itself. Admittedly, though, there was also the transfiguration of the known, the flash that illuminated a cocked eyebrow, a glance, an inflection, and flared up into love, consuming the dross of casual friendship in the blaze of passion.

Out of sight, in the shadow of a tree or in a parked car halfway down the block, the lover lurked and stared and stared as if drugged at the house wherein the beloved actually slept, ate, and showered like any ordinary mortal, unaware of being edged all around in blinding phosphorescence.

Our teachers struggled against it. The purpose of love, they explained, was marriage and parenthood, and passion was the worst possible basis. Our partners should be selected for community of interests, similarity of background, sound health habits, reliability, maturity, responsibility with money, and everything else that was prosaic, suburban, and deadly. We shuddered with dread. Better no future at all than a future so gray.

Better to disembowel ourselves like Mark Anthony, or just lie down and die for love like Barbry Allen.

Today I drive past as the local high school is letting out and hundreds of students clot the lawns and sidewalks, some alone, some with a friend, most in chatting groups. Nobody walks with his arm around another; nobody is holding hands. Groups drive off in cars, radios blasting cheerfully; the songs don't mention love.

News from college campuses is similar. Back when coeducational dormitories were first introduced, elders gasped; surely this meant that passionate love affairs would replace scholarship and the whole student body would waste its expensive university years gazing into one another's eyes and sighing. Wrapped in each other's arms, they would fail to get up for their eight-o'clock classes; they would doodle the beloved's name in their blue-covered exam books and fail the course; they would elope in their junior year.

They didn't. The millennial young are nothing if not pragmatic and keep a steady eye on their future careers. By all reports, campus sex is a brief and occasional matter called "hooking up." Recently five male freshmen and sophomores at Yale threatened to sue the university because of its requirement that they spend their first two years in coeducational dorms. They found the presence of the opposite sex intrusive. For their own part, the females are surging back to the women's colleges once considered all but extinct. They found the opposite sex too aggressively competitive in class.

Once their careers are launched they will form relationships, however brief. These seem to die gentle, natural deaths, ending not in stormy tears, broken hearts, and bitterness, but by mutual agreement, continuing platonically so that some people's social circles consist almost entirely of ex-relationships. Most, if they're lucky, will progress to longer relationships, called "committed," and finally, when the time seems ripe, to premarital counseling. This is a fast-growing industry and at least eleven state legislatures have considered making it a prerequisite for the marriage license, since divorce costs the nation billions of dollars a year. The couple fill out and compare lengthy questionnaires on their goals, values, and expectations, though not on how they feel about each other. Then they receive instruction on conflict resolution, communication, problem solving, and active listening skills; marriage is no job for amateurs. While they discuss possible domestic situations, videotapes in the laboratory record their body language and voice tones and monitors measure their heart rates and the stress indicators in their blood and urine, pinpointing future problem areas. If, after all this, both parties are still willing, they can proceed to the prenuptial agreement and start interviewing caterers. Love may be in a sorry case, but marriage still supports a wide variety of professional and service industries.

Sex, in the meantime, has gone solitary. Spokesmen for the homosexual world declare that it's the very keystone and essence of their nature to have literally thousands of "sexual contacts," each affair lasting roughly as long as it takes you and a stranger to ascend from the lobby to the fourth floor in an elevator. Among heterosexuals, recent academic surveys show that today's Americans, married and unmarried, lead skimpy-to-sluggish actual sex lives, but telephone sex is a $2 billion-a-year business, and sales and rentals of pornographic videotapes have doubled in the past five years, becoming a flourishing business twice the size of major-league baseball. The average American household in 1997 watched six porn videos. When you consider the number of households in which mom and dad collapse from exhaustion as soon as they've turned on the dishwasher and don't watch any porn videos at all, this means that some of us are watching rather a lot of them. The enthusiastic bloom of pornography on the Internet has forced itself onto legislative agendas.

It seems we like love well enough as long as it doesn't require human company. It's been suggested that we feel threatened by the press of crowds around us and fear that if we unchained and cracked the door to let one person in, the whole howling, clawing mass of population would pour stampeding in after her and trample us.

The Greeting Card Association reports that its topselling valentines are, in descending order, addressed to teacher, spouse, child, grandchild, parent, and friend. A quick check of my local drugstore does reveal a "sweetheart" shelf, somewhat shorter than "nephew/niece" or "brother/sister." It's nice that husbands and wives get almost as many valentines as schoolteachers, but didn't the occasion start out as something sexier? Whatever happened to Cupid? Maybe in ten years time we'll be sending our stockbrokers valentines.

If nobody falls in love anymore, does it matter, and if so, is it a good or bad thing? What was it all about, anyway, and why did people find it so important, and how does the world look without it?

Literary love, once fit for big guns like Hemingway and Fitzgerald, Shakespeare and Tolstoy, has gone lowbrow and been consigned to the back alley of

140

paperback romances resold by the sackful for a dime apiece, while respectable books examine the love between the protagonist and his or her interesting self, who often resembles the author. The ups and downs of courtship, once considered the basic plot, gave way to anatomizing the long, slow souring of marriages. The only shining passions in our novels are the remembered, unconfessed first loves of homosexuals. Hundreds of songs have fallen silent because their names—"Love Is All You Need," "Love Makes the World Go 'Round," "I Can't Give You Anything but Love"—are as inscrutable now as pterodactyls singing. Hollywood, once the native soil of romance, has replaced it with special-effects sea monsters, space aliens, disasters, and exotic violence, the love interest pushed into a corner or confined to a single scene of vigorous sex. Television doesn't lend itself to love stories and spends its fiction time with high-speed crime, medical emergencies, and situation comedies in which the sexes forever make war, not love.

Even the phrase "making love" has dropped from the language, replaced by the depressing, impersonal "having sex." Can it be that the awful words we use now have castrated our feelings? The word "lover" now almost always appears with a nonhuman object—animal lover, bargain lover, seafood lover—but surely Launcelot never called Guinevere his significant other. "I think I'm entering a relationship," besides being hard to write sonnets about, lacks the heart-lifting hopefulness of "I think I'm in love," not to mention its accompanying air of deranged radiance. The young, I hear, refer to kissing as "sucking face." Do the words just reflect our apathy, or did they help cause it?

Was ignorance a factor? Do we need to hear about

passion in order to expect it, like poor Emma Bovary? Love without role models loses status, and few people under fifty have heard of Tristan and Isolde, Abelard and Heloise, Porgy and Bess, Dante and Beatrice, Heathcliff, Cyrano, Othello. Because the fate of nations is no longer rocked by love, who today would even believe that Antony and Cleopatra's romance brought the ancient kingdom of Egypt crashing to its knees and set the emperor Augustus on his throne, or that Troy was under siege for ten years because Paris couldn't resist the face that launched a thousand ships, nor could Menelaus let her go? Who remembers that Charles Parnell, the once-mighty nineteenth-century Irish Nationalist leader, was felled because he loved a Mrs. O'Shea? Even the heartbreaker of our grandparents' generation, Edward VIII, who threw away a kingdom to be with his love, has been tilted to look merely neurotic, perhaps codependent. The hanky-panky our modern politicians commit is trivial and hasty. They're too busy for love.

Maybe we all are. Stendhal says quite firmly that "solitude and leisure" are "indispensable for the process of crystallization."

In his cranky 1822 masterpiece, *On Love,* he lays out his crystallization theory, based on bare, scraggly, twiggy branches left in the salt mines of Salzburg and pulled out some months later

> covered with brilliant crystals: even the tiniest twigs, no bigger than a tomtit's claw, are spangled with a vast number of shimmering, glittering diamonds, so that the original bough is no longer recognizable.

I call crystallization that process of mind which

discovers fresh perfections in its beloved at every turn of events.

It took time. He outlines the seven steps of falling in love, passing from interest, to speculation, to hope, the pounding heart, the dampened palms; the first crystallization and the obsessed musings on the beloved's charms; then doubt, the uncertainty of being loved in return, even despair; then a resurgence of hope and the second crystallization that seals one's fate. Stendhal felt that a love so patiently constructed would last for perhaps ten or fifteen years, after which we assume both parties would have become inseparably attached by other ties.

Obviously if, on the evening they first meet, they take a cab to his apartment and spring directly into bed, in the morning they will be only their flawed selves, untransfigured by the diamond salt crystals of love. Maybe they'll go on to have a relationship, but they needn't expect it to shimmer or themselves to glow with perfection in its light. Stendhal makes it clear that where matters were too quickly and easily arranged, as among savage tribes and ancient Romans, love never got off the ground. Anticipation, suspense, and doubt, kindled in idleness, blasted the fires into their white-hot glow.

In the 1960s a vocal fringe group rebelled against what it considered social oppression and took to copulating casually with each other in the name of freedom. In the '70s, spokeswomen for the feminist movement took up the cause and it moved into the mainstream. What was once a rapturous culmination became political therapy expressing liberation; to be in love with one's mattress-mate was reactionary, a throwback to the bad old days of submission and social brainwashing. The orgasm, previously a kind of footnote benefit, was celebrated and dissected and all but deified until it came to stand alone. Sex passed from rite to right and became a solitary exercise that happened to call for an assistant.

Now, with the VCR and the Internet, assistants are no longer required. Call it a kind of personnel downsizing brought on by automation. Certainly it saves an enormous amount of time, compressing into minutes what once took months, and time is always in short supply.

What was this thing called love, and should we mourn it?

Certainly it carried with it a full share of misery, and few present-day disappointments compare with the old-fashioned broken heart. Its roots go way back. Ovid, writing two thousand years ago, speaks of the curative water of a certain well, and says, "All lovers of old went thither on pilgrimage, that would be cured of their love pangs." Washing in the River Senelus was said to help too. In 1621 the scholarly Robert Burton devoted nearly 200 pages of his masterpiece, *Anatomy of Melancholy,* to remedies for heartbreak, and cites a certain rock in Greece, Leucata Petra, as having cured many famous lovers, some of them mythological. He recommends bloodletting and hellebore, a slightly poisonous but popular herb also used to cure fits, madness, and worms, but deplores "illegal" remedies like witchcraft.

Certified psychologists assure us that no one ever committed suicide from thwarted love, only from unmedicated depression and low self-esteem, but if Ricky's self-esteem was low it's hard to see why. He was the flower of our high school, star athlete, top student, in face and form noticeably godlike, and in

144

spite of all this, a genuinely nice fellow. His love was a class ahead of him, and had gone away to college in the fall. In the spring she wrote saying that they had better just be friends. Suicide attempts in such cases are said to be only a plea for attention, a feint to fetch back the faithless, but Ricky shot himself in the temple quite accurately and had no further use for attention, or even for Lois.

His wasn't the only death I've known, and one man was in his forties. There were always some wormy chocolates in the heart-shaped candy box.

On the practical level, love could be a costly distraction. Neither the unhappy lover, haggard and whey-faced, nor the happy one, stunned with joy, was easily engaged by lesser matters. They found the society of those unconnected to the loved one a torture of boredom. The grades of students and the bottom lines of businessmen suffered; they kept talismans in their desk drawers, lipsticks and pencil stubs and crumpled napkins once touched by an angel. Whatever recalled the beloved—a whiff of perfume, a car of the same make and color—brought on palpitations. The hours or days between now and the next encounter were a weary Sahara to be slogged through somehow. It was hard on the health; people in love ate badly, if at all, and lay awake nights nursing their obsession. They forgot to answer when spoken to. They kept losing their car keys.

Tolstoy describes a classic case.

> He knew she was there by the rapture and the terror that seized on his heart. She was standing talking to a lady at the opposite end of the ground. There was apparently nothing striking either in her dress or her attitude, but for Levin

she was as easy to find in that crowd, as a rose among nettles. Everything was made bright by her. She was the smile that shed light on all around her. "Is it possible I can go over there on the ice, go up to her?" he thought. The place where she stood seemed to him a holy shrine, unapproachable, and there was one moment when he was almost retreating, so overwhelmed was he with terror. He had to make an effort to master himself, and to remind himself that people of all sorts were moving about her, and that he too might come there to skate. He walked down, for a long while avoiding looking at her as at the sun, but seeing her, as one does the sun, without looking.

Then, later,

Levin was wondering what that change in Kitty's expression had meant, and alternately assuring himself that there was hope, and falling into despair, seeing clearly that his hopes were insane.

From today's vantage point, love can seem like a debilitating plague for which no cure was ever found but that mercifully, after millennia, died out on its own.

It had its points, though. By comparison, our postlove lives seem a trifle pedestrian. Once even the possibility of being transformed, however briefly, by its amazing grace gave an eagerness to our daily journeys. It may even have served a social purpose, since anyone who concentrated so intensely on another human being must realize that he himself was not the world's only

146

inhabitant, and possibly even his neighbors were people, too. Not lovable, necessarily, but human.

As a palliative or painkiller it had no equal, since it forced everything but itself out of focus. As Romeo put it, "Come what sorrow can / It cannot countervail the exchange of joy / That one short moment gives me in her sight." Heroin, I understand, has the same effect. It may be worth noting that the decline of love and the rise of recreational drugs, the uppers, downers, and hallucinogens that mimicked the path of romance, happened at the same time.

Love improved sex. Even the most unadorned and standardized sex, combined with love, produced a jolt. Currently, to judge from the Internet and the new specialty magazines and newsletters and equipment shops and cable channels, plain sex is no longer worth doing and needs a lot of seasoning, with sadomasochism leading a crowded and growing field of kinks and fetishes formerly considered psychopathic. Love provided its own seasoning.

Everyone recognized it as the one possession supremely worth having, and worldly goods or their absence paled beside it: "For thy sweet love remember'd such wealth brings/That then I scorn to change my state with kings." This was a pretty subversive concept, since the health of the economy depends on us wanting plenty of worldly goods, but at times people really did find love more fun than writing a check for a BMW.

At times it handed out flashes of a blindingly pure joy quite unrelated to other forms of pleasure. Stendhal called it "apparently the most rapturous happiness obtainable on earth." For those who have never been there, it may be impossible to explain.

T. and I, after a sleepless night of love, staggered blearily forth and caught a bus toward our respective offices. The bus was crowded and we were jostled apart in the aisle. Over the shoulders of strangers, our eyes briefly connected, and I would have fallen down if I hadn't been wedged in the crowd. Various writers have tried to describe this moment, usually by comparing it to a massive jolt of electricity, but that sounds painful. Others mention an explosion of interior light so intense that nothing ever looks quite the same afterwards, but that sounds too passive. I have no description to offer, except that it lasted for perhaps a full second, and in the decades since I haven't run across anything worth trading it for.

Writing in 1822, Stendhal was confident that within a hundred years physiologists would figure it all out and explain it to us. They didn't, and now it seems they needn't bother.

RADIATORS

IN THE BEGINNING WAS THE FIRE, AND THE FIRE WAS good. If you could roll aside the other sleeping bodies and get close enough, it kept you from freezing to death. It needed constant feeding, and when the wind changed it smothered you with smoke, and sometimes it got loose and burned down the whole forest, but it was better than nothing.

Eons rolled by, and then we invented the house, and built into it a special nonflammable site for the fire and, quite a long time later, a passageway called a chimney so at least some of the smoke could escape. If you were ill or very old, you got to sit close enough to the blaze so that half of you was hot, while your other half and the rest of the household froze. In consigning one's elderly relatives to the care of others, a place by the fire was usually specified. Snow-covered travelers were rushed to the fireside to melt, and then backed politely away so as not to block the heat.

In considering human history, the wonder isn't that we invented so many things but that it took us so long to think of them. It wasn't until the end of the eighteenth century that we realized we could warm the whole room by bringing the fire away from the wall and enclosing it in a tile or metal box, with a pipe to usher the smoke outside. Even with an east wind gusting, the new stove didn't smoke, and it was three times as efficient, fuel-wise, as the fireplace, though only half as romantic and no fun to watch. The fire inside no longer provided any light, but that was a small price to pay; for the first time the whole family could be warm simultaneously. Ladies backed up to the stove, as they had to the fireplace, and lifted their long skirts discreetly to its delicious rush of warmth. The teakettle simmered amiably on its top and cold hands were rubbed together in the trickle of steam. Life was good.

Finally, the tail end of the nineteenth century brought the culmination of our trials and errors, the joy of our winters, and the pinnacle of our ingenuity, the radiator. It was clean and it smoked not; from its parent in the basement it delivered unto each room a measured, steady blessing of heat. Its pleated shape was friendly to the eye; those in my parents' house sported the ghost of a stamped flower design, blurred by decades of paint, and dainty, higharched feet. As the autumn nights drew in, it hissed and clanked its reassuring promise: winter is coming, but not to worry.

Wet mittens were dried on it, diffusing a wooly smell. The one in the front hall had been boxed in under a wide window seat, and here we threw our coats and jackets, being as a family constitutionally averse to coat closets, and when we put them on again to face the outdoors, lo, they were preheated for us, and not Solomon in all his glory enjoyed such luxury. When we came in again shivering, we huddled over the nearest radiator and pressed our cold hands to its warm face. When January's dry air chapped our lips, we threw a wet towel over it or, in more formal areas, hung a tin envelope of water down its back to moisten our rooms. Radiators maintained a steady temperature, holding warmth even while the furnace was off, modestly dispensing their measured flow of comfort, like grandmothers.

It is not in the nature of mankind to recognize perfection and leave it alone. Having achieved the perfect homeheating system, we scrapped it and moved on. Was it the interior decorators, complaining that they wanted to put a couch along that wall instead of the radiator? Or was it our sudden insistence on summer cool as well as winter warmth? For millennia before the 1950s, it had never occurred to us that we were entitled to live in the same temperature all year round, but once air-conditioning had been invented and spread out beyond the movie theaters, it became a God-given right. The bedroom window unit was not enough; besides being hideous and blocking the view, it didn't do a thing for the rest of the house. We must replace our trusty radiators with a convertible furnace that works all year, delivering its product by means of air forced through aluminum ducts in, or attached to, the walls and ceilings. "Central air," it's called, and who now would be without it? Once we have it, the outdoors seems as threatening in summer as in winter, and we tend to spend most of our days sequestered from the open sky, once considered appropriate penance for only the bloodiest criminals.

In winter, the new system is inferior in every way. It's noisy; it's intrusive; it blows on us and makes our skin flake and our hair straggle. It stays on until we're uncomfortably warm, then goes off until we're uncomfortably chilly. If the intake vent is within half a mile of the smoke alarm, the smallest sizzling steak or even a lighted candle sets off hideous shrieks and howls of impending doom. It provides an ideal delivery system for dust and mold allergens and the common cold.

We can't warm our coat or dry our mittens on it. It offers no grandmotherly source of instant warmth. When we come in half-frozen, we can only stand in the room waiting for the passive air to thaw us. (There's the hair dryer, but it makes a dreadful racket.) No radiator waits for our glad embrace; not even a fireplace or stove offers a warming spot. Just air, invisible, impersonal, and slow to comfort.

You might ask what business we have coming in frozen anyway, since children no longer play outdoors and civilized adults have driven home in their heated cars and into their heated garages, whence they stepped into their heated kitchens, and don't even need a winter coat any more, let alone a waiting radiator.

You're probably right. Still, it seems that our world has buried yet another member of the physical family. Another benign household spirit has tiptoed from the room.

A friend of mine bought an old house with radiators, real radiators. The system, long neglected, needed professional help. He called the local heating guru and

151

was told that the last man who understood radiators had retired the year before, breaking as he went the last link to the days of direct heat, the place that waited to warm us, reaching back to the caveman's campfire.

HOMOGENEITY

I LIVED FOR A YEAR—I FORGET WHY—IN RURAL western Denmark, surrounded on all sides by Danes. They all looked like Danes. They all ate Danish herring and Danish pastries; they drank Danish beer and Danish aquavit. They were all officially Lutherans. Though not notably patriotic in the modern warlike sense, they remembered their country's history and fairy tales, felt warmly about the royal family, and thought of themselves as Danes. When they met another Dane for the first time, they already knew his essentials and most of his virtues and vices and childhood memories. When they looked out the window at night, they knew all the sleepers around them were dreaming Danish dreams. At parties they all sang the same songs.

I was much in demand socially and taken about and displayed as a curiosity: someone different, who spoke only ten words of Danish, and those clumsily. Someone who didn't even know how to skin an eel.

Home again, I got off the plane in New York and was dazzled by the variety of people swarming. People in a full spectrum of shapes and skin colors, gestures, temperaments, voices. It was an adrenaline rush. I was energized, and felt sorry for my Danish friends condemned to the monotony of each other. I was back in America, land of many peoples, and I looked on it and found it good.

I was younger then, and more easily excited by strangeness. Now I'm not so sure. Is it even a country at all we've got here, in any but the crudest geographic sense, or is it more like a deregulated world's fair, with clusters of people in ethnic costume fighting over space to pitch their tents? How are we supposed to feel at home in a place like that?

We're urged to value diversity, appreciate diversity, cultivate diversity. To surround ourselves with persons of every imaginable race, religion, sexual orientation, and country of ethnic origin and call them brothers and compatriots. Alas, it doesn't come naturally, to us or any species; when an ant meets a beetle, it just shrugs, but when it meets a different kind of ant it tears its head off. The unnaturalness of diversity is obvious from the number of children's books trying to sell it: *Janey and An Woo Are Friends; Billy and Ahmed Play Ball Together.* In the illustrations, as in television commercials, the playing children are an orchestrated rainbow of ethnicity, all laughing merrily together. (A few generations ago the message was class rather than kind, and rich children were shown being nice to poor children and inviting them over for tea. That probably didn't sell either.)

We were always the world's refugee camp, but we settled in clumps. The Indians who migrated here before us clumped, and considered themselves primarily Mohawks or Crees or Apaches or whatever; sometimes they traded amiably and sometimes they scalped each other. The European settlers clumped. German farmers gathered together within *heil*-ing distance of each other and built their own church and school. English Quakers gathered to build a meetinghouse and a school of their own. Puritans huddled close enough to monitor each

153

other's bedroom windows. Catholics went here, French Huguenots there. Scandinavians moved into the northern plains where the winters reminded them of home and built Lutheran churches and cooked the food of the homeland. Cities grew to contain their Irish neighborhoods, Germantowns, Chinatowns, Little Italys. Jews established cities within cities, where they could send the kids to Hebrew school and trust the kosher butcher, and the neighbors understood Yiddish. Free blacks set up their own villages and elected their own mayors, and later moved into the cities and lived in their enclaves there, to the latter-day grief and horror of liberals, who took it for granted that they'd rather be living with whites.

We came here as refugees or slaves or adventurers, to a country where we didn't recognize the leaves on the trees or the sounds of the birds, and collected familiar customs and faces around and made ourselves at home. Here, as in the old country, when a young man came to call on your daughter, there was usually nothing surprising about him. He spoke your language and his manners were your manners. (Sometimes your daughter, bored with the sameness of it all, ran off instead with the stranger who passed through town. The stranger—the outlander of unknown parentage and unfamiliar ways—who passes through causing havoc is a standard figure in American tales.)

For a while, communities ran their own schools, such as they were, and the teaching reflected the community, and the children reflected their parents. Then, in the 1830s, the idea of public, tax-supported schools took root in Massachusetts, and spread through New England and on beyond, meeting various degrees of resistance, then as now, to their lack of religious dogma and, of course, the taxes. They undertook to teach all the children the same things, and they became the thread that sewed us together: we learned the same things in school.

Since we'd been a British colony, and so many of us were of British descent, schoolchildren were instructed in what was considered our heritage. As long as there's a clear majority it makes sense—at least to the clear majority—to teach its canon to all, and never mind that the British Empire was racist. Children had to identify King Arthur and the Battle of Hastings and Magna Carta. Much of western European thought had filtered down from Greece and Rome, so children were expected to remember that the Parthenon was on the Acropolis and not the other way around, and that all Gaul was divided into three parts. The ambitious learned Latin and French, historic vessels of Western culture.

At the midpoint of the twentieth century, my public high school required me to spend a full year on American literature, starting with Jonathan Edwards ("The God that holds you over the pit of hell much as one holds a spider or some loathesome insect over the fire, abhors you, and is dreadfully provoked; his wrath toward you burns like fire"), and a full year of English literature, starting with *Beowulf*. The first year included some poems by Emily Dickinson and the second some poems by Christina Rossetti, but other than that it was wall-to-wall dead white males of western European descent, much of it splendid stuff and well worth knowing. It wasn't until late in the 1960s that the authorities realized nobody wanted to read stuff written by people unlike themselves, by people who were born a different color or far away or a long time ago, because what could they know about us and our personal problems?

Once, the mainstream was broad and compelling and we were all expected to swim in it. Nobody complained. Immigrant parents wanted their children—as long as they didn't forget the family recipes or marry someone peculiar—to become as thoroughly American as possible, complete with Anglo-American history from the Anglo-American point of view. And what we learned in school was what we had in common. We were all, as the corporate brass would say, playing in the same band. In later life, the offspring of wildly different backgrounds could say, "You had to read *A Tale of Two Cities?* So did we. God, what a bore!" When we mentioned Trojan horses, or fiddling while Rome burns, or crossing the Rubicon, everyone knew what we meant.

Now the mainstream has shrunk and its tributaries multiplied. Thirty years ago, "minority" was a polite word for blacks, unless the subject was religion, when it meant Jews. Step by step they were accommodated. Harriet Tubman and Frederick Douglass entered the canon, and Black History Month was born, and schools closed down for Martin Luther King, Jr., Day. The Christmas pageant was replaced by the winter festival and "Silent Night" by "Frosty the Snowman." Then things got complicated.

The country has been swamped by a growing tide of new immigrants, and these are mostly from Mexico, Central America, the Philippines, Korea, and Southeast Asia. As of 1996, over six and a half million Americans were born in Mexico and well over a million in the Philippines. Many of our new people simply aren't much interested in going mainstream here. Like previous settlers, they settle in clumps, but the clumps tend to be more cliquish and numerous and mutually hostile. Nationalities don't want to be collectivized; Koreans don't want to be called Asian, since they have nothing in common with Cambodians, and Salvadorans say they're Salvadorans, not Hispanics, and certainly not Americans, whatever that may be. They all circle the wagons. Many of their homelands now offer dual citizenship, and they can go back to their roots to vote.

Even among those here for generations, roots, rather than America, now mean identity and stability. Roots, it's understood, grow in the far-off soil of one's ethnic origin, from Ireland to Ethiopia, and any struck down in the new dirt are held to be purely expedient and draw no useful nourishment. Roots must be officially respected, even the roots of the Hmong-American family, speaking a Sino-Tibetan dialect nobody else understands, who recently sacrificed a sheep in the living room to heal their ailing daughter.

Gladly or not, the earlier immigrants planned to become Americans, but many of the new ones aren't even resigned to learning English, and fights break out here and there over what language teachers should teach in, since it's tyrannical to expect the speakers of other tongues to learn a new one, as if we thought English were somehow superior to Urdu.

Quite shortly, in much of the country, the minorities will be in the majority, as they already are in several states. What, then, shall we do to the curriculum? What of the autumnal story of Thanksgiving, Pilgrims and Indians and colored cutout turkeys taped to the kindergarten windows; chirpy little voices singing, "All is safely gathered in / Ere the winter storms begin"? What are Pilgrims to a Cuban child? Turkeys to the Chinese? What's a harvest to the children of

157

Vietnamese fishermen, or winter storms to a Puerto Rican?

What can we teach at all? Can we decently discuss the Declaration of Independence, when Jefferson owned slaves, or the American Revolution, when Washington did, or the Constitution, when Madison did too? Why should Abraham Lincoln be more important than Emiliano Zapata or Mahatma Gandhi or Nelson Mandela or Chairman Mao? But how would learning about Mandela—or Lincoln, for that matter—nurture the cultural roots of a Filipino? Is it wrong to teach American history at all, if it means neglecting the history of Central Africa, Laos, Colombia, Haiti, Pakistan? What does Greco-Roman culture matter to our new children, and why should they consider the works of Michelangelo? Can we give equal time to Confucius, Plato, Mohammed, Martin Luther, and Martin Luther King? Equal time to both Sunni and Shiite Muslims? How can we offer Beginning French if we can't also offer Hindi and Swahili? And what on earth are the children to read?

Battles over the correctness of the reading list have been escalating ever since *Huckleberry Finn* was banished for the *"n"* word, but once it was a relatively simple matter of black and white, male and female. Now nobody can be excluded. As of this writing, matters have come to a boil in San Francisco and blows are being exchanged over the books, with quotas demanded for every ethnic, religious, and national element of the student body, plus the gay and the lesbian, quite irrespective of literary merit or general interest. San Francisco has been trying—one of the ten classic works on the recommended list is by someone named Ng—but not trying hard enough, as half the books are by "European Americans" (the fact that Arthur Miller is Jewish and Tennessee Williams gay doesn't count in their favor), and only twelve percent of the students match them. Since only ten books are at stake and the students represent eight ethnic groups and at least two sexes, the problem seems insoluble.

It isn't, though, and indeed the answer is already up and running. Forget Pilgrims and turkeys, Shakespeare and Gettysburg. We will teach the children math and science.

Math and science. They have, while we were busy elsewhere, become synonymous with education. Wherever education is the subject, the words are spoken reverently. (It's understood that "science" doesn't mean botany or anthropology or any of those squishy, old-fashioned subjects with field trips. It means computers.) Shall we build a new magnet school? It shall be the Frederick Douglass School of Math and Science. Math and science shall catapult our children into the global economy of the twenty-first century and give them all terrific jobs distributed without bias. Shall our children be measured against those of other lands? They shall be tested in math and science, not sonnets or choreography, and their scores shall come out just ahead of Zimbabwe's. Therefore we must try harder, fill their every moment with math and science, scrap last year's computers and buy new ones and more of them. A school district near me has given every single pupil a personal laptop, so there need be no gap between home and school computer, and everyone can work on the school bus.

The young must still learn to read—*The Complete Idiot's Guide to Windows 95* runs to 385 pages—but as soon as they've mastered the necessary words, it's back to the algorithms. Is a child praised as "creative" or "imaginative"? That means he can dream up new uses for technology. It's the wave he must ride to the future, and best of all, it's culturally neutral. A cultural vacuum, in fact. No child studying calculus can complain that his roots aren't being respected, and no one remembers whether Newton owned slaves.

When they grow up, their generation, like the generations before, will have learned the same things. However, the children in Iraq and Japan and Brazil will also have learned exactly what ours have learned. Math and science do not an American make, and as a source of comfort and companionship and identity, they're pretty chilly. Not likely to replace the warm sense of being, at heart, Cambodian.

Meanwhile, in the school cafeteria, Janey and An Woo, Billy and Ahmed, are not eating lunch together. The children and grandchildren of the melting pot clump together at their separate tables and each cleaves to his own.

The earlier immigrants cleave, too. Sometimes they pack up and turn their backs on all that exciting polyglot diversity. It's said that for every new immigrant who comes into the immigration-magnet points and unpacks, a native-born white leaves. Most move so far out into the suburbs that they don't even try to find familiar customs and live inside the walls of their houses and cars. Others move to places like Idaho and Montana, to the towns and small inland cities where children still cut out Thanksgiving turkeys and read *A Tale of Two Cities* in school.

Far from the seething urban stew, at the high school's homecoming assembly, they will choke up

160

when the choir sings *"Thine alabaster cities gleam / Undimmed by human tears."* In their hearts they can see America, their America, peopled from sea to shining sea with those like themselves and their neighbors, where everyone thinks American thoughts and dreams in English. It may not be exciting, but it feels like home.

A cosmopolitan city is a brave and stimulating thought, especially from a distance, but the fast-approaching cosmopolitan country is too splintery to think about at all.

PLAYING CARDS

WHEN I WAS NINE MY AUNT PEGGY TAUGHT ME TO play poker. She called it a survival skill.

Probably few families worry today that the children will blow their allowances drawing to a busted flush, but that was then: people played cards. In the evenings my mother prowled among us riffling a deck and asking, "Anyone want to get their socks beat off at gin?" A woman totally uncompetitive, who cared not a fig for winning on any other field, she played gin rummy with blood in her eye. If through a wild stroke of luck one of us beat her, we had to make it the best two out of three, and invariably fell. She enjoyed blackjack and fantan, but gin was mother's milk to her. When she was old and tired and ill, a few mean, hard-fought hands of it brought the sparkle back to her eye.

The boys in the back room played poker. Down at the firehouse, the firemen played pinochle between fires. In the parlor the ladies played bridge, and the week's hostess served snacks appropriate for the game, mostly nuts and raisins sold as "bridge mix." In the nursery the children played hearts and slapjack, and the boys practiced the fancy shuffling that would be admired in their later lives, cards leaping smoothly through the air from hand to hand. Alone in furnished rooms, life's discarded played solitaire. Cards were played in the cafés and bistros of Paris and the salons of Venice and the beer gardens of Munich and the dining rooms of Minneapolis. They were a universal pastime and international language; travelers in foreign lands could socialize with the natives without needing any words beyond "knock with four" and "raise you ten."

Cards were a useful social ploy. When you moved into a strange neighborhood, someone would invite you over for "an evening of cards" with others in the area, so much less taxing than an evening of unaided conversation, and by midnight you would know each other, for better or for worse.

Playing cards, you were together with companions, but you weren't their only source of entertainment; you were occupied, but not too distracted to chat; you were in competition, but only in the saloons of the old West and the glory days of Monte Carlo was it a matter of life or death—the old gang's weekly poker night was usually a matter of nickels and dimes, and the permanent gin rummy game in the employees' cafeteria was a quarter of a cent a point, with the tab kept running basically forever—nobody ever paid up, but the sense of money at stake elevated it from time killer to sport. Sometimes the game was so absorbing that the players forgot to chat, and sometimes the chat was so absorbing they forgot to play, but both were always options. The only other sport that can make that statement is croquet, but you can't play croquet in January, or even in the rain.

In 1887, to settle arguments, someone named Hoyle compiled a book, *Official Rules of Card Games (for pleasure and relaxation . . . PLAY CARDS!)*. It was published by the United States Playing Card Company and reprinted every year thereafter and sold so many copies they ran out of zeroes. "According to Hoyle" made its way into the language, meaning to follow life's official rules. Hoyle included the basic forms for basic games, and variations and offshoots with names like skat, sludge, garbage, spit-in-the-ocean, and "honeymoon bridge," modified for two players and conjuring up the bleakest of scenarios.

Purists were sniffy about variations. My little grandmother, having grown up in the old West, would fold up her hand if the dealer called for something uncouth, like one-eyed jacks wild. "If you're going to make a *circus* out of it . . . " she would say, and retire to bed. She played five-card draw or seven-card stud in their pristine form, and nothing else.

Cards weren't always respectable. They came to us along about the thirteenth century, from somewhere in the mysterious East, and seem to be descended from the tarot deck, which survives in our modern Joker, once the tarot's Fool. They were banned and burned all over Europe, acquiring a luster of forbidden secrets. The whiff of black magic clung to them, and well through the twentieth century fundamentalist preachers raged against them; even when no money was wagered, they were the devil's placards, worse even than dancing, another once-widespread sin. This made them especially alluring to the young.

They were held to pave the path to ruin, and sometimes they did:

First down to Rosie's and then to the card house—
Shot in the breast, and I'm dying today.

Jack o' diamonds, Jack o' diamonds,
I know you of old.
You've robbed my coat pockets
Of the silver and gold.

Nothing stopped them. Versatile, adaptable, portable, and irresistible, they made their way through the whole social spectrum until even the most virtuous household kept poker chips in a drawer, beside the dog-eared copy of Hoyle and the many decks of devil's placards.

The backsides of cards being necessarily blank, they cried out for purely decorative touches. In 1392, Charles VI had three decks made for him in "gold and diverse colors." Around 1450, a German artist and engraver known to us only as The Master of the Playing Cards created his lone masterpiece, a deck of illustrated cards most wondrous to behold. Twentieth-century card makers ran riot with a gallery of illustrations, ranging from reproductions of Great Art to ladies in indecent poses. Children collected them, knocking on doors and wheedling the jokers from the neighbors' decks, and set up a value system for trading them; I remember that Gainsborough's *Pinky* and *Blue Boy* were at the top, worth many a lesser picture, while geometric designs could hardly be given away.

Then, after entertaining us for seven hundred years, cards faded out of our daily life a decade or two ago, at least at the amateur level. Anyone yearning for a spot of blackjack must now take a plane to Las Vegas or one of the new gambling casinos springing up and raking it in all over, and lose money under professional supervision.

The traditional, long-running Friday night poker game was somewhat friendlier and much less expensive.

For casual gambling, the lotteries and the slot machines have taken over our hearts and wallets. They're fast, and we're in a hurry here. They have no tedious rules to remember. They're convenient; pick up a lottery ticket where you buy the morning paper. They're easy. No skills are required. Glassy-eyed, the rows of women at the slots hypnotically repeat the simple gestures: insert, pull, whirr, clank, insert, pull. To the uninitiated it looks less interesting than counting sheep, but the women persevere until the grocery money's gone, apparently having forgotten how to stop.

Cezanne's *Card Players* still hangs on the wall, the players still poker-faced and intent on their hands, and children must wonder what they found so absorbing. At century's end, except for a few gray-haired surviving bridge groups, it is quite thinkable to run a well-equipped household without a copy of Hoyle or a single deck of cards in the whole place. I suppose the fundamentalist preachers and the sixteenth-century popes would be pleased and feel we had taken a long step on the road to Heaven, but I'm not sure that was why we gave them up. Scrabble had made heavy inroads earlier, but the final collapse may have had more to do with the VCR.

It's probably not important. Probably no great cultural tradition has perished in the decline of card playing. It was just another one of those things, like the parlor piano, that brought us together, and caused us to visit our neighbors and invite them into our houses. Just another ritual we had in common.

Hoyle has finally, after a hundred years as basic education, gone out of print. Rooting around, I found my own ancient copy, under two boxes of poker chips. Mice have eaten most of the cover, and stirring the chips produces clouds of dust. I should throw them away.

TELEGRAMS

HE WORE, AS I DIMLY REMEMBER, A DISTINCTIVE brown uniform. He rode on a bicycle, tinkling its bell. He knuckled the front door and called in through the letter slot, "Western Union!" and all hearts stood still. With shaking hand the yellow envelope was torn open and the short, wide, yellow message in capital letters was unfolded, to triumph or tragedy. MISSING IN ACTION or EIGHT POUNDS TWO OUNCES STOP BOTH DOING WELL.

Bad or good, the telegram's news was, by definition, important. Sender and receiver alike felt important. The neighbors leaned from their windows and wondered. Now all our news wears identical clothes; the ringing phone can mean a death in the family or a stranger selling aluminum siding. A letter with our name and address handwritten in blue ink can mean a long-lost lover resurfacing or Publishers Clearinghouse telling us we may already be a winner (the postage is the giveaway—lovers pay full freight). Letters marked Urgent! Open at Once! are either Publishers Clearinghouse again or a politician in need of campaign funds. The fax is basically utilitarian and means business, though sometimes it runs amok and transmits book-length manuscripts, a landslide of pages spewing forth while we wring our hands and pray for the paper-roll to run out. E-mail is more frivolous and lends itself better to trivia; forwarded strings of dreadful jokes, sales pitches, chain letters, and midnight maunderings cling to it like lint. Bosses abuse it by thinking up lists of boring rules and sending them to everyone.

Nothing now arrives with the pure impact of the Western Union boy.

Perfecting telegraphy occupied the techies through much of the nineteenth century. In 1861, Western Union constructed the first transcontinental line, and by the end of the Civil War a durable cable finally crossed the Atlantic. Through the first half of the twentieth century, telegrams flew 'round the world like birds. People who could almost have shouted to each other, or at least picked up the phone, sent telegrams instead. Telegrams were chic. They were glamorous in a way the phone has never been; upgrade it how we may, the phone is not romantic. It's confrontational. It catches the recipient off guard and demands immediate response. The reply-paid telegram saying I LOVE YOU STOP WILL YOU MARRY ME gave her time to think it over, while bombshells like ARRIVING HOME AFTERNOON TRAIN STOP BRINGING NEW WIFE DARLENE STOP KNOW YOU WILL LOVE HER provided a cooling-off period with the sender safely out of reach.

In England in particular, phones seem to have been considered vulgar, maybe because of their invasive nature, and relegated to the servants' hall so the cook could order groceries while the upper classes sent each other telegrams.

Novels and plays revolved around telegrams. In E. M. Forster's *Howards End*, a telegram arriving minutes too late kicks off the whole plot. In Evelyn Waugh's *Handful of Dust*, a young man who has been vaguely invited to come down some weekend sends a cleverly timed wire announcing his arrival just as he leaves to catch the train, too late for his hosts to forestall him, and the plot takes it from there. In plays, women ripped open telegrams stage center and fainted dead away. Their husbands pried the crumpled sheet from the nerveless fingers, clasped their foreheads and cried "Good God!" and read it aloud to the audience.

The literati on both sides of the ocean rejoiced and telegrams became an art form. As the compressed discipline of the haiku lends itself to musings about blackbirds, the compressed discipline of the telegram lent itself to wit, of which brevity is said to be the soul. The wags of the Algonquin round table wasted long hours composing memorable telegraphic jabs, and Noel Coward's became classics. George Bernard Shaw wired Winston Churchill:
FIRST NIGHT OF MY PLAY NEXT WEEK STOP TICKETS RESERVED STOP BRING FRIEND IF YOU HAVE ONE. Churchill wired Shaw: UNABLE TO MAKE FIRST NIGHT STOP WILL COME SECOND NIGHT STOP IF THERE IS ONE.

Business boomed during the urgencies of World War II, and by the 1950s Western Union had two million miles of wire in its nationwide network, serving 30,000 offices that handled over 200,000,000 telegrams a year.

What happened? Few corporate empires and few cultural traditions crash so fast. By the '60s, message central had dwindled into a convenience for sending money to ne'er-do-well relatives stranded in gambling dens. The streets were swept clean of messengers, and if you did get a telegram, some starchy-voiced person called you on the phone and *read* it to you, which seemed curiously indecent, and several days later the hard copy arrived by mail. Why bother?

In 1970 a friend of mine was musical director of a show opening on Broadway. Of course I knew my duty:

how could a show open without the traditional blizzard of break-a-leg telegrams? Self-consciously, mindful of possible display backstage, I labored mightily over my message, and was well pleased. With difficulty I contacted one of the last vestiges of mighty Western Union. I explained. She sniffed. No way, she said, could they guarantee delivery by opening night, or even predict delivery time within forty-eight hours. I blinked like Rip Van Winkle.

The greeting-card business has rushed into the vacuum, and it's just as well, as they provide professionally prewritten words we're now too busy to write ourselves. Once the telegrams arriving for birthdays, bereavements, weddings, and graduations could be stuck into a picture frame or taped to the refrigerator or pasted in an album commemorating the event. Now we get Hallmark cards on which our relatives have written "Dear Uncle Elmer," on top of a printed verse that says

> Thinking of you
> On this special day
> And how much you mean to us
> In every way!

with "love, Lisa and Bill" at the bottom. Mostly we don't paste these in albums. They're not the same.

CHILDHOOD

FROM THE PRESIDENT OF THE UNITED STATES DOWN to the least welfare worker, everyone agrees that one of our most urgent national problems is supervising children. Organizing them into teams. Telling them what to do. Keeping them busy. Watching them at all times. With so many mothers off working in offices, children after school and on summer vacations are a clear and present danger to themselves and others. If not closely controlled, they may meet up with each other unsupervised. Children without an adult standing by will form gangs and use drugs.

Even during the school day they need to be kept separate, and many elementary schools have abolished the time-honored custom of recess; newer schools are built without playgrounds. Recess, even with teachers on guard, led to children hobnobbing together on their own, learning God knows that. Picking up extracurricular customs of their own. Anarchic customs.

Children are bad for each other. This is a given.

A fairly new given, actually. The past is rarely what it looks like in the light of current problems. As we now see it, all mothers once spent half their days and all their summers staring fixedly at their young and regulating their behavior. In truth, most mothers have always had other things to do, and from the dawn of time until about twenty years ago, the first duty of children was to stay out from underfoot and not bother the grown-ups. The second duty was to be home by dark or by dinnertime, whichever came first. Other than that, the grown-ups simply didn't much care what the children were doing. They felt it was none of their business. A parent taking too keen an interest in the children's lives was said to be "smothering" them, and probably spoiling them, too.

In the children's world, grown-ups were shadowy bystanders. Richard Hughes, in his eerie revelation of childhood, *A High Wind in Jamaica,* writes,

170

If it would have surprised the mother, it would undoubtedly have surprised the children also to be told how little their parents meant to them . . . Actually, the Thornton children had loved Tabby [the cat] first and foremost in all the world, some of each other second, and hardly noticed their mother's existence more than once a week.

Middle-class families used to be larger, and older kids were expected to keep an eye on the younger ones, and got blamed if they hurt themselves. Except in heavy rain, all of us were sent out of the house to "play," which in those days meant anything we felt like doing, for as long as we felt like doing it. Out there in the world, we encountered other children, and formed a fluid neighborhood group. The group was based not on affection or community of interest but simply on proximity: we were children, and available to each other, and so we bonded and set forth in search of something interesting to do.

City children drew hopscotch patterns on the sidewalk, played death-defying tag on fire escapes and kickball in vacant lots, where they wounded their hands and knees on broken glass, and stole apples from pushcarts. Catholic and Protestant children lined up on opposite sides of the street and insulted each other's religions.

Country children tried to ride cows, dared each other to tease the bull, and marooned a calf in the bell tower of the church. They learned how to knock a rabbit out cold with a slingshot and how to build a fire. The older ones taught the younger ones how to swim by pushing them into the river and how to fish by making them dig worms, and sent them up the neighbors' trees to steal apples.

Suburban children, of which I was one, played hide-and-seek up and down the backyards of the block. We dug a hole in the flowerbed to see what was really on the other side of the world and, disappointed at finding nothing but dirt, buried someone's little sister in it. We learned to blow up a paper bag and pop it with a fist, and to whistle piercingly through a grass blade pressed between our thumbs, and to burp at will. We formed secret societies with complicated rites involving blood and passwords. We dealt out rough justice among ourselves, ranging from ostracism to physical violence; invoking adult intervention, called "telling," was unforgivable. We pretended to be fighter pilots, spies, and characters from comic books. We made up plays and gave circus performances and tried to charge admission, but nobody would pay. In winter, noses running freely, we dragged our sleds for miles looking for the most dangerous hills. If we needed a bathroom or a drink of water, there would be an available source nearby, but no grown-up in residence there could be considered supervisory.

By any modern standards we were shockingly ill equipped. Should it interest us, in the spring, to play some baseball, we had a couple of backyard trees for bases, a headless broom for a bat, and a dead tennis ball we found in the hedge. The smallest child was forced to be catcher, a brutal job often involving rosebushes. When we got bored or mad, we quit and did something else. Any civic-minded citizen today, seeing us so pathetically deprived in such a comfortable suburb, would have hauled us straight off to Little League. We would have hated it.

There were Boy Scouts and Girl Scouts, and most of us were pressured into joining, however briefly. They turned out to be an extension of school. Nothing that involved a grown-up telling us what to do, and how, and when, could possibly be called "play." One by one we dropped out and returned to our anarchic pursuits.

We built rickety tree houses that collapsed and pitched us to the ground, knocking us breathless. We nailed a pair of roller skates to a wooden crate, stuffed a sibling into it, and pushed it down the hill, and it would hit a curb and fall apart. Still, we had made it ourselves. "A poor thing, but mine own, sir." Making things under supervision, on a rainy day at some dismal summer day camp—place mats, hand puppets, bead jewelry, birdhouses—was not creation but tyranny. (Probably grown-ups shouldn't attempt to foster creativity in children, since the line between fostering and bullying is pretty thin, but just try telling that to a grown-up.) Making our own messes, we took the measure of our powers. If we needed to know something, we asked an older kid, since we weren't segregated by age as children are now.

We learned from other children. We learned where babies come from ("Eew, yuck!"), and many vulgar songs, some of ancient lineage, and dreadful riddles ("What has four wheels and flies?" "A garbage truck!"). And starting as the least of the least, in street and playground, we inherited the pervasive, age-old underground culture of childhood.

Who knows how old giant step and Mother, may I? and prisoner's base were? Ring-around-a-rosy was believed by some authorities to date from the Great Plague. London Bridge is falling down may have grown out of the destruction of London Bridge by King Olaf and his Norsemen in the eleventh century. Its game, with the children ducking under the two pairs of arched arms, went back to the early fourteenth century. Gone now. Vanished almost overnight. Here and there an earnest kindergarten teacher may try to resurrect them, but this marks them as just another lesson; some things had to be transmitted from child to child down the centuries or the magic leaked out of them. Besides, I suppose children steeped since infancy in the adult-generated culture of cute, of *Sesame Street* and Disney and Seuss, would find them puzzling, especially as presented by a teacher.

If children were an isolated tribe of Brazilian Indians who had so abruptly lost their ancient traditions, professors would rush in to try to resurrect them, but it wouldn't work. The links are broken.

Teenagers had no ancestral culture to lose, since they were only invented in the middle of the twentieth century and the Oxford *English Dictionary* still doesn't carry the word. Back then, as we grew older, we rode away on our bikes and abandoned our childish pursuits. We went looking for work, paid work, before and after school and on weekends, because it made us feel important. Any five-year-old could go to school, but work conferred grown-up dignity. Bagging groceries, running errands, delivering newspapers, pumping gas, and peddling magazine subscriptions, the boys saved up their quarters to buy a derelict car, rescued from the knacker's, and have it towed home. Thenceforward they spent their spare hours underneath it, sneakered feet protruding, or tipped buttuppermost into its maw, and haunted junkyards for bits and pieces until by the time they were old enough for a driver's license they had the thing running, after a fashion, and were king of the world, and could drive their worshipful ex-playmates around the block and pretty girls home from school.

Back in their old neighborhoods, the eight-year-olds had turned into ten-year-olds, and bullied and instructed the six-year-olds, and the underground world of children went on.

Until at some point toward the end of the twentieth century, it stopped.

Four or five times a week I drive through a pretty little town surrounded by green fields. Its houses are mostly modest and crisply painted, and their lawns are broad and kempt, and trees and flowerbeds flourish. The speed limit for the occasional car is 25 miles an hour. Crime is unknown. Nothing about the town has changed since 1950, or possibly 1900, except that it seems to have been abandoned. Its sidewalks are empty. Its silence is broken only by birdsong. Once or twice a week I see a middle-aged citizen taking a mandated walk. On a Saturday I may see a bicycle, but it's always ridden by an adult male in helmet and spandex, looking determined. Never a child. Five years ago there were still some old signs saying Children At Play, but someone's taken them down.

I know from the statistics that this town is fairly bursting with children and its elementary school bulging out of its classrooms. It's slightly sinister to think that hundreds and hundreds of children can be so effectively hidden, as if they might all be locked in the basements. They aren't, of course; people around here are most particularly tender and careful of their children. Either they're safely in their rooms facing television or computer, or they're off being safely supervised on softball or soccer field, or in karate or gymnastics classes or basketball clinic at the community center, or practicing with the under-eight swim team. Anywhere but loose.

Parents and coaches and the sponsors of youth sports call it "playing," but previous generations of children, noting the presence of an adult with a clipboard and a whistle around his or her neck, would have called it slavery and scattered to the four winds. The current children don't seem to mind. Never having tasted freedom, what would they do with it?

Animal behaviorists consider the activities of young mammals to be a preparation for adult life, as playing kittens stalk and pounce on each other as practice for stalking prey. Considered in this light, today's children get the best possible training. They divide their nonschool time between television and supervised competitive team sports. Television trains them to want advertised products, which means they must work hard in school in order to get good jobs in order to buy advertised products. (It inspires some of them to go out and steal advertised products, but they're a minority.) The sports produce ideal employees, obedient and cooperative, with a bloodthirsty competitive zeal on the team's behalf.

Still, imagine Mark Twain trying to write a new *Adventures of Tom Sawyer*. Adventures? The kid's not even allowed to carry a pocketknife, let alone camp out without a scoutmaster. Least of all, run into such unauthorized companions as Huckleberry Finn.

They'll do well in the new century, our kids. Probably even recess won't be missed, though looking back it seems to me that the most useful lessons of childhood were studied at recess—hard, chewy lessons about luck, unfairness, power and helplessness, defiance and conciliation, and revenge. Maybe they won't be needed anymore.

Certainly the lost lore of childhood won't be needed. It never did have any market value in the grown-up world. Sometimes I find myself trying to remember, though. Seeing the new moon over your left shoulder and making a wish; wasn't there something you had to say? And warding off bad luck and evil spirits, you closed your eyes and turned around three times, chanting something, but what? Pre-Christian, I suppose. I can't remember, and I can't ask my children because they never learned. Gone now. Pity. Even in the twenty-first century, it might have been good to keep handy.

SNEAKERS

I HAVE JUST SEEN AN AD, AND I REJOICE TO REPORT that sneakers are still being made. Not only that, but the same firm makes them that made them back when people wore them; the same firm still gallantly sending out an entire range of sizes, even though I, their last customer, only wear an eight. Thus might a manufacturer of sterling reputation continue producing skirt hoops or ox yokes, waiting for their time to roll around again.

Now as then, sneakers are made of lightweight cotton canvas with rubber soles. Aside from their laces they have no moving parts, and nothing in them is covered by patent. They would, given half a chance, still serve their original purpose of providing traction and persuading the feet that they are wearing no shoes at all—the foot's idea of heaven—while protecting them from bee stings and sharp gravel. They were sometimes called tennis shoes, and reckless as it seems, I suppose people were allowed to play tennis in them, back when tennis was played on lawns by the intense young hero of an E. M. Forster novel and pretty girls in Edwardian dress who never used foul language or hurled their rackets at the bystanders, and laughed when they lost.

In schools, sneakers were required wear for gym classes, lest our leather soles scratch the shiny basketball floor. They were kept in small airless lockers and by the end of the semester they smelled horrific; we called them gym shoes to distinguish them from home-based sneakers, which led a freer life and smelled better. They came in two styles: the standard, which stopped well below the anklebone and was white, at least for the first few days; and high-tops, which were black and marked the wearer as a serious male student of basketball. When fouled, sneakers were thrown in the washing machine. When retired from more formal pursuits, they were worn laceless to walk in the creek or wash the car.

Generations padded softly past in sneakers. We wore sneakers for everything from horseback riding to square dancing to lying around in the grass, and nobody told us not to. We wore the same sneakers our forebears wore in 1865. American manufacturers were asleep at the switch.

Then, with a roar, they woke up. They looked around. They saw an America newly inspired to exercise itself, and they saw it bending and stretching, jogging and pedaling and hiking, all while wearing the same pair of five-dollar sneakers. They sprang into the breach. They retooled the factories; they invented, trademarking and patenting as they forged ahead; they researched; they developed; they advertised, and hired wagon-loads of sports stars to wear their products; they created a separate specialized sports shoe for every conceivable physical activity; and, most wondrous of all, they persuaded ordinary people they needed these devices badly enough to pony up a hundred dollars a pair.

By the mid-1980s they were on most of the feet in sight, and by the mid-1990s they were fetching their happy makers over $12 billion a year. Otherwise well-dressed businessfolk wear them to the office. Children wear them to preschool. Adolescents put nothing else on their feet, even for funerals, and when breaking into shops they steal them before any other item. White-haired grandparents trudge the malls in them. Admittedly, they're hideous; nobody ever said they weren't. If the slender sneaker of yore was the gazelle of the shoe world, the new sports shoe is its rhinoceros. A sneaker on steroids. Even the smallest sizes are the size of inflatable lifeboats; they need to be, to accommodate all that science within their bulges.

Flip through the simplest outdoorsy catalog. The cheapest, a shoe to be worn for "fitness walking" and only $60, comes with C-CAP midsole and compression-molded EVA orthotic. Here's a cross-trainer, which someone told me was to be worn while using exercise equipment; it has an exclusive Cantilever concave sole. For more money I can get a multicourt cross-trainer with an Abzorb heel and forefoot, or one with a midfoot stability bridge for energy release. Running is more expensive; I will need a dual-density DuoMax midsole to control velocity of pronation and a lightweight graphite Rollbar for rearfoot stability, more like a prosthesis than a sneaker. Light hiking is fancier yet and tops a hundred dollars, with inverted gusseted tongues, full-length Phylon midsoles, Dri-Lex lining, Air-Sole units, and thermoplastic heels. Sneakers for riding a bicycle are so specialized that, off-bike, you can barely limp across the room in them and they wear out in three months. To go out in a boat, you need four-way grip and hydrophobic uppers. For "casual wear," or just hanging out with the gang, the Air Massage system incorporates a polyurethane outsole with enclosed air bubbles, a steel shank, and a forefoot flex zone. And if you think you might want to shoot a few hoops or hit a few balls, a separate specialty model awaits you for each.

And what of those who exercise as rarely as possible? Even we sometimes need to get from one place to another, and for this we must have the peerless M1064. It looks rather like a sneaker, but don't be fooled; it's been scientifically engineered for walking around in— unlike lesser shoes maybe designed for playing Scrabble in. A pair costs $230, but what can we do? We can hardly stroll shamelessly across the backyard in sneakers designed for the StairMaster.

I've been told, though I'm not sure I believe, that one of the most costly and coveted models has lights set into the heels, for the convenience of anyone chasing you down a dark alley.

I was visiting friends who lived above a river that had recently enjoyed a glorious flood, and we all wanted to go poke along its ravaged banks in search of treasure. Unfortunately I'd come in sandals, least adaptable of footwear. No problem; my hostess had an extra pair of light-trail hikers that would be the very thing. To go with them, she lent me a pair of sports socks, or maybe light-trail socks, specially padded and as substantial as an old-time sneaker. I sat down and struggled into this gear, marveling. The shoes had high, fatly padded tops that, once I'd been helped to fasten them up, seized and held me like giant clams trapping an unwary diver. I tried to walk. My ankles were clasped immovably, and somewhere beyond them my feet were encased in cement like those of a Mafia victim en route to the East River, weighing forty pounds apiece. "That's *support,*" said my hostess. "Support's the most important thing. You'll get used to it."

To prove it, she and my host waltzed out of the house wearing similar architecture and headed for the river. I lurched after them like the statue of the *commendatore* in *Don Giovanni.*

The riverbank was steeply eaten away by the floods, slippery with mud and strewn with boulders. With no control from the knees down, I started to tilt dangerously forward toward the rushing waters. Panicking, I threw myself backward to safety on a gravel patch. These things were out to kill me. I sat up and began to deconstruct my footwear, latch by lace, and managed to pull my prisoners out of it, and then wrenched the light-trail socks off as well. I stashed the equipment on a rock and followed my friends down the bank, using only what had come in my original package. Though it winced occasionally on sharp stones, it turned out to be highly advanced scientifically, crafted entirely from organic materials, lightweight and supple, with purpose-designed heel and forefoot pads. The synchronized tarsals and metatarsals of the arch gave it strength and acted as a lever. The transverse arch across the metatarsals helped distribute weight, while the heel bone supported the longitudinal arch. As a unique feature, it was equipped with five flexible extensions for improved gripping and balancing. The ankle structure flexed in all directions, compensating for uneven light-trail terrain. Best of all, it didn't cost a nickel.

All afternoon we dug for treasure, coming up with the usual bottles and cans, a bicycle wheel, a perfectly serviceable barbecue grill, a belt buckle depicting (I think) General Custer, the chassis of a wheelbarrow, a picnic bench, cartridge cases, a pineapple, a trash can still attached to its Park Service chain, and a drowned raccoon. And a sneaker. A plain canvas sneaker, with a hole worn over the big toe, much used, mud-brown now and evidently of great antiquity.

Reluctant to leave it decaying, I rinsed it off in the river and carried it back with me and set it to dry on the porch. It survived the flood. All may yet be well.

DEPARTMENT STORES

FOR A TREAT, MY GRANDMOTHER TOOK ME SHOPPING with her at Woodward & Lothrop in downtown Washington. Downtown was where you went to shop, and for us who lived in the suburbs, the trip was part of the treat, and included lunch. For Grandmother, there was no store but Woodie's for pure respectability. She disapproved of any emporium that held more than two sales a year; she lived frugally on a schoolteacher's pension, but she felt that promiscuous discounts and markdowns were a rowdy way to do business and a sign of shoddy wares.

In nice stores, reduced-price merchandise was not suffered to disfigure the selling floors but was hustled down to the bargain basement, where amenities were few and the lighting dim and the sales help unattractive. "Bargain hunter" is a compliment now, mark of a canny consumer, but back then it was an insult. Nice people, if they couldn't afford the asking price, saved up until they could, or did without. Chasing after a better deal showed a lack of pride and breeding. It smacked of haggling. Of gypsy horse traders.

Grandmother had shopped at Woodward & Lothrop for chairs and lamps and dishes as a bride, and then for a crib and baby clothes for my mother and aunts, and then school clothes, and then wedding dresses, and then yarn to knit me a baby blanket, and she treated it as a second home, bigger and more elegantly furnished than her own but just as welcoming. She knew every alcove and nook, and which way to turn when we got off the elevator. She and the saleswoman in the yard goods department addressed each other by name. Grandmother asked searching questions about materials and workmanship, and examined each prospective purchase closely, and turned garments inside out to check the seams. Then we had lunch in the tearoom, with a hot fudge sundae, and went home. The next day the square brown truck pulled up to our door and a cheerful young man in a brown suit brought in whatever it was we'd bought, however small and weightless. The lettering on the truck was gold. "Woodward & Lothrop," it said proudly, once upon a time.

One by one they close down, the queenly old downtown department stores. Their customers, many of them elderly, line up on the sidewalk for the final markdowns. They bid farewell to their old friends among the sales staff and condolences are exchanged. Lifelong customers weep. Stock boys and sales clerks weep; they tell reporters it was like a family, that they'd worked there for twenty-two years and the pay wasn't great but they loved it; they'd never considered changing jobs. The newspaper prints an editorial elegy and a clutch of doleful letters. "Washington without Woodies is like the Mall without the Monument," one woman laments. San Francisco without I. Magnin like the bay without the bridge; Philadelphia without Wanamaker's like independence without the declaration. All gone in the space of a year or so. Sudden vacancies gaping in the identities of cities.

The grand facades stand blind and empty. What's to be done with them? Offices? A convention center? A warren of chain stores identical to those all over the country; stores with no roots in the city and no interest in it beyond their sales figures? The wrecker's ball?

We shall not look upon their like again.

Grown, I moved to Philadelphia, where Wanamaker's was waiting for me. Woodward & Lothrop was lovingly known as "Woodie's," but Wanamaker's got all four syllables—its ceilings were too lofty for nicknames and the pipe organ in the Grand Court too grand—but it was never unfriendly. The least of us citizens were welcome. In the days of my deepest poverty I always walked through the first floor from Chestnut Street to Market, and felt rich. The air in there smelled rich, of Italian leather and Swiss chocolates and French perfume; I could breathe it for free. The store was freshly landscaped every season, like a continually changing garden, and the decorations lightened the step and the heart. I remember one spring when the first floor was a festival of buttercup yellow, with real yellow tulips blooming everywhere and, suspended over the counters, immense white wicker birdcages full of real yellow canaries spreading song out over the hosiery and handbags. (Somebody told me later that a person from the display department was deployed to come in early and check the cages and replace any birds that had perished overnight, but there's always a seamy side.)

A distinguishing mark of the grand old stores was the amount of space and time and money they lavished on that which brought in no revenue. The ladies' room was a stately marble hall furnished with comfortable chairs and couches and tables laden with glossy magazines, staffed by clucking motherly attendants with needle and thread and extra buttons, hairpins and towels and aspirin and Alka-Seltzer and, for all I know, scalpels and sutures. The bronze Wanamaker eagle, mascot and logo, beloved of the city, used up the central spot in the Grand Court, space enough for several merchandise counters. It was enormous, with benches set all around it, and here Philadelphia met each other by prearrangement, and set forth for lunch and shopping. The floor-to-ceiling pipe organ had cost the founding fathers a bundle, but its lunchtime concerts were free.

The old stores seemed to deck their halls with merchandise for our pleasure rather than their profit; we were honored guests at the bountiful mercantile table, and great pains had been taken with the feast spread before us, not from mercenary motives but to give us a sense of the grand possibilities of the world. They shed a graceful glow over the prosaic process of acquiring things, so that stocking up on the children's socks and underwear was an act of elegance and dignity. The elevator rose solemnly through layers of offerings, each announced by the elevator operator as he slid open the brass-grilled doors: Better Dresses, Lingerie, Gentlemen's Haberdashery, Mattresses and Bedding, Children's Shoes, Pianos, Rugs and Carpeting, and whatever else the heart could desire.

As the suburbs burgeoned around midcentury, branch

stores were opened in them, but these were strictly for emergency shopping. Low, windowless, concrete boxes surrounded by parking lots, with neither grace nor glamor, they were not courts into which you entered with praise, but only to grab some badly needed item and leave again. The branches were drones; the downtown store was queen.

Once you'd entered through the discreet swish of its revolving doors, there was no pressing reason ever to leave. Wanamaker's hosted a full-service post office down on the mezzanine; an apothecary shop that carried the astringent toilet water my grandmother had used; an optometrist; exotic delicatessen; an ample book department; watch and jewelry and shoe repair and a piano tuner and a beauty salon and a bridal consultant. (Harrod's in London was so excited by Lindbergh's transatlantic flight that it opened an aviation department and taught its customers to fly.)

The stores deep-rooted in their home cities cherished their reputations for service and quality; the dissatisfied could go straight to the top and bang on the executive doors. The problem would be set straight at once, from the highest level, with apologies, even if the customer was obviously lying, and goods returned for full refund even if they'd been worn to a party. Who now, angry at one of the multitudinous Macy's stores, can march into the offices of Federated and complain? Who knows who Federated is and where he lives?

Christmas was the glory season for the stores, and again they seemed to be doing it all purely for our pleasure. Every well-brought-up child was taken to see the animated windows, walking slowly around the block with long pauses to watch the elves building toys, Santa trimming a tree, Santa's sleigh with galloping reindeer, furry animals ice-skating, trains winding through snow-scene mazes, and maybe, in those incorrect days, a nativity scene with sheep and shepherds. It's hard to imagine today's children, blessed as they are with such exciting entertainment, gazing in awe at a store window, but gaze they did, back then. I took my own children, every year, and every year the store served up fresh delights.

As my grandmother had taken me, so I took my daughter Christmas shopping, dressed in her best bib-and-tucker. Children in the great stores were always peculiarly well behaved. Come to think of it, so were the grown-ups. The crowds in the weeks before Christmas thronged thickly, but they were peaceful and merry crowds, and even the harried salespeople, many of them grown gray in loyal service, managed to smile. The display department toiled late hours to outdo the glories of previous years. One year Wanamaker's commissioned its own exclusive teddy bear, white, with a sweet face and a red bow, in several sizes and astounding quantities. They were everywhere, mounded in great pyramids all over the first floor and peeking out from every nook, the joy being in the reckless abundance of bears, bears in their thousands, suggesting a limitless world of innocent pleasures to hug. The littlest bears hung on the enormous annual tree—a real tree, smelling of forests—and the biggest bears lolled underneath it. For some reason the effect was magically pleasing, and that year the shoppers all shopped smiling.

The toy department blossomed and spread itself out over the adjacent departments, and "Jingle Bells" was played on real bells, and the path to Santa's bailiwick was a winding journey past animated display cases, with mimes and jugglers and pretty girls dressed as gnomes to while away the wait.

Then there was lunch in the tearoom. The restaurants and tearooms of the great stores produced no vulgar smells to coarsen the atmosphere, no garlic, no hamburger grease. The special was probably creamed chicken in a patty shell; the tea sandwiches were cut in triangles and filled with ladylike watercress and creamed cheese and pimento. At Wanamaker's the tearoom overlooked the Grand Court, and at lunchtime the great organ played carols and local choirs came from all over to sing, and during the concert, as you looked down on the crowds, all shopping came to a halt. However rushed and busy the shoppers, most on their lunch hours from work, they all stood still and listened.

Certainly people still take their daughters Christmas shopping, but I doubt if they dress them in their prettiest finery now and tie a ribbon in their hair. Perhaps they don't even consider it a treat. They drive the long spokes of traffic through the suburbs past mile after mile of stripmalls, where discount stores clear to the horizon sell nothing but reclining chairs, nothing but light fixtures, nothing but jeans, nothing but toys. They don't deck their halls with real velvet ribbon or real holly, the music is piped in, and the sales help is cross, but the prices, they all insist, are unbeatably low.

The scramble for bargain gifts is a fixture of the season now, but only a little while ago it seemed crass beyond words and a slap in the teeth of the holiday spirit. I remember my first encounter with it, a friend newly in love and anxious to give her boyfriend an extravagant and memorable gift. A sweater, it was, a special sweater she knew of, made of something exotic like unborn alpaca fur, and it cost a fortune. For a week she trudged from store to store comparing prices until finally she was satisfied that she'd made the best deal. This was perhaps twenty years ago, and at the time I thought it was bizarre, to resolve on a wildly extravagant gesture, and then go looking for the cheapest possible wildly extravagant gesture. Didn't this rub some of the bloom off? Not for him, of course, since he wouldn't know, but for her? She didn't see it that way, though, and now no one does.

The joy of bargains has grown on us. We flock to stores with names like BiRite and SavMor, feeling that a weakness in spelling will be reflected in a comparably feeble pricing. Somehow we've convinced ourselves that if we buy something we don't need for ten dollars here instead of twelve dollars there, we're two dollars richer instead of ten dollars poorer. Accordingly, we spend many more hours of our precious time shopping, seeking the lowest prices, and behind us the grand old stores with their marble bathrooms and real holly close their doors forever. With their passing, we're left face to face with our naked determination to have more things than anyone else and pay less for them.

My daughter still remembers Christmas lunch at Wanamaker's, my sons still remember the dancing gnomes in the Christmas windows, but their children won't. Impossible to explain to them that people once walked into the great stores of the cities and smiled, not at the bargains, but because we were happy to be there. Being there made us feel like ladies and gentlemen, and so, for the moment, we were. No chain store called SavRite can be quite so civilizing.

PRANKS

TWO YOUNG MEN—THEY WERE COLLEGE FRIENDS of my mother's—were offered the rare chance to buy, quite legitimately, a surplus municipal park bench, and naturally they jumped at it. They had no particular use for a park bench, but they were sure they could think of one, and presently they did. Under cover of darkness they smuggled it into a municipal park well supplied with identical benches and then, one on each end, they carried it back out along the lighted walkway. Slowly and keeping under the streetlights, they came to the city sidewalk. Just as they'd hoped, the cop on the beat spotted them and hustled over to make the arrest.

"But officer," they chorused in tones of injured innocence, "this is *our* park bench." The bill of sale in all its correctness was presented. The policeman, baffled and angry, retreated.

That's all. That was the whole point and purpose, carefully planned and triumphantly achieved. No doubt the two men told their grandchildren; no doubt their grandchildren were even more baffled than the cop: why would anyone bother to do such a thing?

The master of Tom Sawyer's school was a heavy-handed disciplinarian, also totally bald under his wig. Tom's schoolmates banded together for revenge on the last day of school, examination day. They enlisted the help of the sign painter's boy, who boarded in the master's house and could do his work when the master dozed off, befuddled with drink as he always was before this occasion.

The evening dragged on with many a recitation. For

the geography examination, the master turned to draw a map on the blackboard, wondering at the titters from the audience:

There was a garret above, pierced with a scuttle over his head; down through this scuttle came a cat suspended around the haunches with a string; she had a rag tied about her head and jaws to keep her from mewing; as she slowly descended she curved upward and clawed at the string, she swung downward and clawed at the intangible air. The tittering rose higher and higher, the cat was within six inches of the absorbed teacher's head; down, down, a little lower, and she grabbed his wig with her desperate claws, clung to it, and was snatched up into the garret in an instant with her trophy still in her possession! And how the light did blaze abroad from the master's bald pate, for the sign-painter's boy had *gilded* it!

Pranks had a long history. The gods and goddesses of ancient Greece, being underemployed, spent much of their time thinking them up. The Little People of the British Isles made careers out of pranks, befuddling the simple farmers and their wives, leading them down strange paths until they were lost, bewitching them into delusions, and instigating rebellion among their livestock. Puck of *Midsummer Night's Dream* causes the Queen of the Fairies to fall madly in love with Bottom the weaver, ass's head and all, purely for his own entertainment. Most folk cultures of the world had a prank-player, a fox or a monkey or Uncle Remus's Bre'r Rabbit, who always scampered away laughing.

Mortals, mostly young and mostly male, turned road signs around to point in the wrong direction and dressed in sheets to hang around cemeteries, alternately giggling and moaning. A favorite of the urban young was laying a wallet attached to a string on the sidewalk and hiding with the other end of the string; when a passerby picked up the wallet it was magically twitched out of his hands. Simple, but satisfying.

It was basic to the prank that it not cause any lasting harm; he who rigged a bucket of water or ashes over a doorway to spill onto somebody's head was in no way related to him who brings a gun to school to shoot his classmates. Neither were pranks vandalism; proper pranks required more creative thought than simply breaking things and provided proportionally more satisfaction. The line between vandal and prankster was clear: the vandal slashes tires; the prankster placed a handful of pebbles in the hubcap, where they produced a harmless but maddening rattle to confound the driver and a whole series of mechanics.

My brother attended a small college in the northern plains where there was precious little to do in the endless winters except watch the freshmen shovel snow. That, and carry a whole classroom's furniture outside and arrange it neatly on the quad and flood it, so that it froze immovably into place and stood there till spring, the lectern sternly facing the snowy desks.

My brother's roommate took a Polaroid shot of my brother emerging from the shower in a state of nature. Then he purloined some stationery from the dean of women's office and wrote my brother a severe note, enclosing the picture and demanding that he present himself in her office at 3 P.M. sharp and explain why this indecent picture was circulating through the chaste precincts of the women's dorm.

Then my brother dyed his roommate's entire supply of underwear lavender.

Then the roommate and some friends carried my brother's Volkswagen up the steps of the administration building and blocked the door with it. The other entrances were buried deep in snow; there was a meeting of the distinguished trustees of the college that morning; there was no way into the building but for the distinguished trustees to crawl or slither from the driver's door to the passenger's door and out the other side.

Then my brother, using appropriate purloined stationery, wrote a stately and regretful letter to his roommate's parents saying that their son was flunking most of his courses, probably due to his heavy drinking.

The following fall, his roommate suborned votes and stuffed ballot boxes and had my brother, who was awkward with the fair sex and had never danced a step in his life, elected Homecoming King, to lead the Homecoming Ball with the Homecoming Queen. (This misfired, as the Queen was a jolly girl who gave him a crash course in dancing, cut his hair, and supervised his formal wear, so that he carried off the evening with dash and flair, disappointing his election committee.)

And so the academic years passed merrily, trading blow for blow. Graduation loomed. At the final hour, my brother obtained his roommate's address book and chose at random a female name from the roommate's hometown. Sparing no expense, he had handsome invitations engraved, requesting the pleasure of the recipients' company at the wedding of the roommate and this female, at her home address.

These he mailed to all their college chums and all the other names in the address book. Then he sent a wedding announcement to the happy couple's hometown newspaper, packed up his belongings, and departed the ivied halls of academe.

Impossible to explain to the grandchildren. Pranks were just one of those things, like whistling or blowing smoke rings or writing limericks, that we did to amuse ourselves, way back when we, like the gods and goddesses of Olympus, were in charge of amusing ourselves.

ICE-SKATING

In *ANNA KARENINA*, THE LOVE STORY OF KITTY AND Levin begins at the Moscow skating grounds, near the zoological gardens. The ice is free and open to the public, and commodious enough for a colorful whirl of Muscovites of all ages. Here we meet Kitty with her dear little muff and her slender feet in their skating boots; Kitty a bit timid on the ice, leaning on the skillful Levin. We know at once that this romance will be a happy one, all purity and light to set against the dark passions of Anna and Vronsky, because nothing ominous happens on the skating ground. As with picnics, where people gather together to slip over the ice, there evil is vanquished and innocence dwells. Or dwelt.

We can hear it in "The Skaters' Waltz" and see it in the paintings from medieval Europe to yesterday's Central Park, pictures of Norwegian harbor, Belgian town, Dutch canal, and Minnesota millpond. They positively twinkle with innocence. Authors from Louisa

May Alcott to John Cheever saw skating as a spiritual cleanser and refreshment for the soul. Before antidepressants, the medical benefits of spending winter days outdoors in whatever light was available, meeting friends, exercising not just painlessly but joyfully, and gulping deep breaths of fresh air far outweighed the odd chance of breaking through the ice and getting soaked.

From roughly 1000 B.C. until roughly 1980 A.D., wherever winters were cold enough to freeze water, people fastened various devices on their feet and rushed out to slide around on it. It was fun; observe the joyful faces in the paintings. Unlike the rough team sports, it was open to pretty girls, mothers and grandmothers and small children. Neighbors gossiped, gliding side by side. Apparently it made the winters jollier than the summers, when the people in paintings toiled in the fields. In marginal climates, everyone hoped for a cold winter, the colder the better, as they still do in the canal-laced, mild-wintered Netherlands, so they could skate. Marie Antoinette loved skating. Even Napoleon gave it a try.

In London, in 1683, a great frost fell upon the town and the Thames froze solid and stayed solid for three months. This sounds like a disaster for a shipping port, but London rejoiced. King James ordered the river swept clean and decorated and furnished as a pleasure park. He invited Europe's most brilliant society to visit him there, and the riffraff showed up too. Horse-drawn coaches ran a regular service down the ice from Westminster to the Temple. Everyone set up tents and made carnival, with plays and puppet shows, bonfires, dinner parties, fireworks, beer drinking, bull baiting, music and dancing, races, crap games, horse-trading, and even a printing press that stamped out people's names and the date as souvenirs. London spent the winter on skates. The diarist John Evelyn called it a "bacchanalia." The cheerier diarist Samuel Pepys, by then a respectable bureaucrat of 50, reported dancing on the ice, probably in one of the quadrilles the king organized.

In Washington, in 1994, a great frost fell upon the town and the Potomac froze solid, but the president failed to organize a carnival and skating was forbidden. Everyone grumbled about the cold and stayed indoors, and the government actually closed down for a few days because it was too cold to go to work.

Freezable water used to be widely distributed. Where it wasn't, resourceful people flooded low-lying areas, even their front lawns, and waited for them to freeze. My sister, riding the public school bus through the countryside, waited with her fellow travelers through December until the day when the boy with the best farm pond stood in the aisle and shouted "The cow walked over the pond!" His father was strict: no skating until the cow walked across the pond. After school that day everyone gathered, and built a bonfire on the bank for warming their hands, and skated till dark, because this was the whole point of winter.

Ten years later, when I was raising children near Philadelphia in the 1970s, creeks still ran free and ponds dotted the landscape, and I drove the children from pond to pond, starting with the shallowest one that froze first, little more than a puddle at the bottom of a field where a morose mule watched us philosophically, and moving on to deeper horizons as winter hardened. Every fall I gathered the outgrown skates from the back of the closet and took them to the hardware store, where the amiable proprietor dedicated a table to the free neighborhood skate exchange; drop off the old ones and poke through the donations for the next size up.

In the city, park ponds froze and everyone flocked to them, carrying thermos jugs of hot drinks. In cities with neither ponds nor canals, indoor skating rinks charged admission to an oval skin of artificial ice, with piped-in music, but it wasn't the same. An indoor skating rink is similar to a high school basketball court, and innocence dwells not therein. The innocence needed real ice under a real sky.

Innocence may have contributed to the downfall of casual skating: it was noncompetitive. The clumsiest amateur had as much right to the ice as the best and fastest. Impromptu and disorganized, it resisted even the most zealous coach trying to forge it into teams or get up a proper race, what with the area all cluttered with lovers and geezers and dancers and toddlers. Ice-skating, nobody won or lost, which is not the American way and possibly a bad influence on the young. People were just out there gliding around enjoying themselves, a shocking waste of time.

In addition to its pointlessness, it came to look dangerous. As the 1980s moved in, people came to see that safety was the highest end and aim of human life, and also that, when safety failed, lawsuits should be filed. Where ice was based on real water, a person could conceivably break through and, in the worst-case scenario, drown. I suppose it happened. I do remember being coached in the rescue technique, laying boards out toward the hole or, lacking boards, slithering on my stomach to distribute the weight, with a backup slitherer at my heels. I don't remember any epidemic of drowned skaters, though, or even a single case of pneumonia. But one by one the ponds sprinkled across country landscape and city park were fenced or drained and filled. I don't know where the morose mule goes for a drink these days, but at least no skater will now break through the puddle and get his feet wet.

Curiously, at the same time, downhill skiing was becoming the rage with the smart set. Unlike skating, it requires bulky expensive equipment and advance planning, reservations, and usually a long trip by car or plane to the designated area, and money, and waiting in lift lines. Before the breakaway bindings came, so many skiers broke their legs that the cast and crutch came to be winter's status symbols, and recently not one but two national celebrities killed themselves skiing into trees, almost simultaneously, but somehow nobody has proclaimed the slopes dangerous and shut them down. I would hate to think this is because entrepreneurs have sanctified them by making money on the operation, but we must admit nobody ever made a nickel by letting folks skate on the creek.

Here and there frozen water still lies open and waiting, but nobody's using it now. Driving in a recent cold winter, I passed a fine, capacious pond a mile or two outside of a Maryland city. It lay spread out in several acres of the profound gray that means it has frozen clear down to bedrock. It was a sunny Saturday afternoon. There was room for cars to pull off the highway. Anyone with a pair of skates slung around his or her neck could have sat on the bank, laced them up, and glided away. Nobody had. Not even the cartoon of Snoopy the dog, muffler flying, clowning it up.

Last summer I stumbled on what looked like a skater's dream of heaven. I was visiting a friend in West Virginia, a state that takes danger a bit more philosophically than some, and we drove on the wild and steep and winding roads past hundreds of ponds.

Around every bend a silvery patch of water twinkled like a coin dropped under its willow tree. The landscape shimmered in their reflected light.

"Johnny Pond-seed passed through here," said my friend.

"And in the winter?" I cried. "In the winter, do people skate on the ponds?"

"Never," he said.

Maybe this is why so many people keep moving south. Not much point in winter anymore.

Skaters have moved from the winter landscape onto the television screen. Hockey, once played by small boys with a lump of ice and the fireplace poker, has gone big business, and now every city must field and televise its well-paid team. Deaf to the call of innocence, the players spend the game attacking and insulting each other and being sent, still cursing, to sit out penalties. It's a ferocious sport, a kind of supervised war, which may explain its popularity with the viewing public.

Watching hockey is a fast-growing sport, and among women watching figure skating has become a religion. Female figure skaters are as goddesses, and no more innocent than goddesses ever were, with their personal problems laid out at length before us. During the Winter Olympics clips of their practice sessions appear on prime time, slipped in between interviews with their relatives. In their competitions, a tumble or the loss of a few percentage points devastates the women of America, writhing helplessly on the couch.

We don't aspire to do it ourselves. People don't look at the victorious hockey players or the gold-medal figure skater, turn off the set, grab the skates, and head for the ice to try it. We understand that skating, proper skating, involves managers, trainers, corporate sponsors, contracts, and thousands of hours of practice. Like singing and dancing, it's not for the likes of us. We're allowed to watch, and we're content.

Holding the wrong end of the telescope to the eye, we can look back through its tunnel into the quite-recent past. There is the portly gray-haired couple skating together, holding hands across their stomachs, matching each other stroke for stroke. There's the toddler, so bundled into its snowsuit it can barely waddle, dangling from its father's hands, feet sliding backward from under it. Here's the young man who compensates for his pimples by doing a shoot-the-duck and a leaping spin, pretty tame stuff to those who have watched the Olympic triple lutz, but the neighborhood girls applaud.

The shallow winter sun dips under and in pairs and groups they take off their skates and leave, until only one skater remains, carving out figure-eights in the thickening dusk.

By sunrise the pond will be drained and filled with borrowed dirt, and by spring a Wal-Mart will open on its site. In the meantime the lone skater leans into his curves, hands clasped behind him, red tasseled stocking cap swaying. The bonfire on the bank has died down to coals. Someone has dropped a mitten.

Dear Reader:

I hope you enjoyed reading this Large Print book. If you are interested in reading other Beeler Large Print titles, ask your librarian or write to me at

Thomas T. Beeler, *Publisher*
Post Office Box 659
Hampton Falls, New Hampshire 03844

You can also call me at 1-800-251-8726 and I will send you my latest catalogue.

Audrey Lesko and I choose the titles I publish in Large Print. Our aim is to provide good books by outstanding authors—books we both enjoyed reading and liked well enough to want to share. We warmly welcome any suggestions for new titles and authors.

Sincerely,